LAMBERHURST
JEWEL OF THE HIGH WEALD
A HISTORY

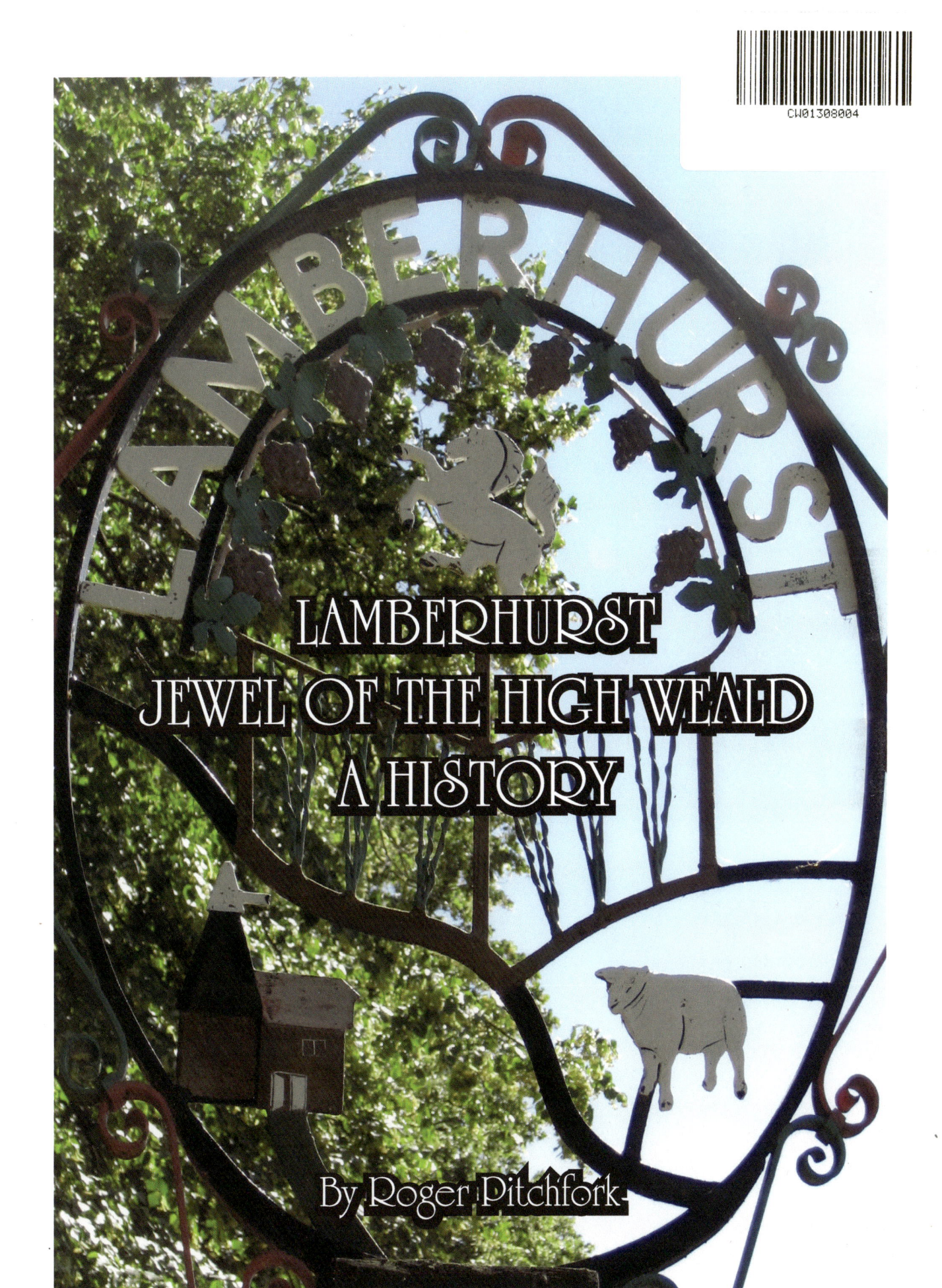

By Roger Pitchfork

Authors OnLine
www.authorsonline.co.uk

An Authors Online Book

Text Copyright © Roger Pitchfork
Cover design by © Jamie Day, Roger Pitchfork

All rights reserved. No part of this publication may be reproduced, stored in a retrieval system, or transmitted in any form or by any means, electronic, mechanical, photocopy, recording or otherwise, without prior written permission of the copyright owner. Nor can it be circulated in any form of binding or cover other than that in which it is published and without similar condition including this condition being imposed on a subsequent purchaser.

British Library Cataloguing Publication Data.
A catalogue record for this book is available from the British Library

ISBN 978-07552-0635-3

Authors OnLine Ltd
19 The Cinques
Gamlingay, Sandy
Bedfordshire SG19 3NU
England

This book is also available in e-book format, details of which are available at:
www.authorsonline.co.uk

PREFACE

I must confess to never reading prefaces as they are normally long and boring.
I believe a preface should précis the book, introduce how it came about and be short, sharp and to the point. So be it.

There are a multitude of references to Lamberhurst in many excellent books and many detailed subject short stories or overall papers, particularly by the late John Moon.

However, after completing a history of the house that my wife and I live in on The Broadway, I felt that the village lacked a book that recorded its history and the development of its industries, in an easy-to-read format that could be used to share with as many people as possible. So this is what I have attempted to do.

The written word is our ancestry, but I also believe the old adage, 'a picture tells a thousand stories';
so therefore, where possible, I have included as many illustrations as I can.

My reference list is long and I acknowledge the research and efforts of my author sources; for this reason, I regard myself not as a soloist, but as the conductor of a large orchestra of talent, in the hope of producing a piece of work that readers will find interesting.

Finally, I wish to record my thanks to the residents of the village, who, although I have not lived here for fifty years and I am very much a newcomer, have been friendly and I regard as my friends: Marjorie Edwards, Peter Sands, Mickey and Brenda and Nick and Julie.

I dedicate this book to my wife Clare; Lamberhurst may be the jewel of the High Weald, but Clare is the jewel of my life.

INTRODUCTION

Lamberhurst is situated in the High Weald of Kent, forty miles south of London.

The soil of the valley bottom is sand, the hills very stiff clay.

The site was evolved over millennia, by the River Teise eroding the upper strata levels of the Weald to create one of the most fertile areas of the entire High Weald; however, it would take time to convert this hidden gem into a jewel.

This erosive action of the River Teise and its tributaries would uncover iron nodules which the Romans discovered in other parts of the Weald, and they developed an iron-smelting industry that was the second largest in their entire empire. But High Weald Lamberhurst remained untouched, and even Roman and Jute pathfinders 'travelling through' would have been rare.

The first regular visitors would have been the early Saxons, who found that the woodlands surrounding the river valley were ideal pannage (feeding) pastures for their swine, but only stayed here during the season.

Soon, competition from illegal drovers necessitated protection and stability and so the Saxon 'Lord of the Manor', who owned the land, built the first timber church and a meeting house, for himself or, more likely, his reeve (representative), and developed a water meadow and encouraged his land tenants from Rochester to move here permanently and establish the first settlement in the valley bottom, close to the location where the two main drover roads in the area intersected and where the best river crossing was for miles around. They began clearing areas of the forest to provide timber and better pastures and named the village as a description: 'soft clay on a wooded hill' or 'a woody place that is suitable for lambing or the pasturage of lambs'.

The Norman conquest transformed the developing community. The new 'Lords of the Manor', whose official seat was Leeds Castle, rebuilt the church and meeting house and built two gist mills on the river, all in stone, and oversaw the development of the village's first domestic industries, baking and cider production.

With the gradual clearing of the forests, the next industry developed: sheep for wool. This was exported in great quantities to the continent, legally or illegally, and financed the building of the first Wealden Hall Houses, utilising the favoured local oak in its timber-frame construction.

Lamberhurst did not stop to draw breath when the wool market collapsed, as Robert Cogger had built his Fulling Mill in the village and was successfully manufacturing Kentish Broadcloth commercially and cattle replaced sheep as the main agrarian activity.

Then followed the first example of industrial vertical integration in the village as the leather industry logically followed the establishment of a weekly cattle market and slaughter-house. A tannery, a curing shop, a dye shop and finished leather goods workshops were established.

Iron manufacture was established at Lamberhurst Furnace and Forge at Hoathly, which produced cannon in great numbers for one hundred and fifty years and swallowed up the local labour market to coppice the woods, produce charcoal, transport the raw materials, man the iron works and to transport the finished goods.

The population grew rapidly in the 16th century, when over twenty different industries were in operation and a minimum of thirteen new Wealden Hall Houses were built and five extended or refurbished.

The county border line was adjusted in 1894, making the entire village in Kent.

Then hop growing expanded and witnessed the arrival of the London East End families to pick during their summer vacation and then beer brewing expanded in the 19th century and chemical manufacture was established in the 20th century.

All that has now gone and the village with it?
On the contrary.

We have the busiest village shop in the area, selling everything from groceries to a dry cleaning service. A bakery to which commuters divert on their homeward journeys to buy its wonderful bread. An entrepreneurial butcher, who takes the supermarkets head on with his unrivalled quality and range of meats. A hairdresser who successfully competes with the up-market salons in Tunbridge Wells. One of the oldest pubs in England. One of the best Italian restaurants for miles around.

And we have history: over one thousand years of it; witnessed by one Grade I and over sixty Grade II Listed buildings and personal visits by three different Kings and Queens of England and by two Archbishops of Canterbury.

The hidden gem is now a jewel for all to enjoy.

CONTENTS

iii	PREFACE
iv - v	INTRODUCTION
1 – 4	PART 1 – THE DENS OF LAMBERHURST
5 – 19	PART 2 – LORDS OF THE MANOR and important activities during their rule
5 – 7	Aethelbald
7	The Bishops of Rochester
8 – 9	Bishop Odo
9 – 10	The Crevecoeur Family
10 – 12	The Archbishops of Canterbury and The Abbots of Robertsbridge
13	Henry VIII
13 – 15	The Sydney Family
15	The Porter Family
15 – 19	The Morland Family
20 – 82	PART 3 – LOCAL INDUSTRIES
20 - 21	Swine Fattening
21 - 23	Water Meadow Farming
23 - 25	Wool
25 - 27	Baking
27 - 36	Corn Milling
37 - 41	Brewing: Cider, Beer & Wine
42 - 45	Cloth Manufacture
45 - 46	Animal Husbandry: Cattle
46 - 48	Weekly Market, Annual Fair & Slaughter Houses
49 - 50	Leather
50 - 59	Iron Manufacturer & Forging
60 - 64	Hop Growing
65	Clock & Watch Makers
65 - 66	Construction
66	Saddlers
66	Hop String Manufacture
67	Chemical Manufacture
67 - 75	Other Retail Trades: Butchers & General Stores
75	Various
76	Historical Chart – Lords of the Manor
76	Historical Charts
77	Historical Location Chart - Baking
78	Historical Location Chart - Cloth
79	Historical Location Chart - Leather
80	Historical Location Chart – Brewing
81	Historical Chart – Occupations 1851
82	Historical Chart – Farms 1881
83 – 84	PART 4 REFERENCES AND ACKNOWLEDGEMENTS
85 – 88	INDEX

PART 1 – THE DENS OF LAMBERHURST

BACKGROUND

Introducing and understanding the 'Dens' is important, as they pre-date the village and their very existence was directly responsible for the initial establishment of Lamberhurst.

Five 'Dens' (which translates to 'woodland swine pasture') existed within this part of the forest of Caesterweraweald (later shortened to Weald) and the oldest dates back to before 747.

One was in Kent, four were in Sussex.

All were located on the high ridges surrounding the village and would have been well-drained forests, unlike the marshes of the valley bottoms.

The Church owned all the dens up to 1066, when they were taken illegally by force by the new Norman Bishop of Leeds, Odo, William the Conqueror's half-brother. He in turn sub-let them to the Count of Eu of Hastings Castle (who held the Sussex Rape of Hastings).

William imprisoned Odo in 1082, took over his Lindhrycg den and passed the other dens to Count Robert of Eu, who subsequently passed them to the Bishop of Robertsbridge.

Immediately prior to the death of William I in 1087, Odo was pardoned and all his lands reinstated.

The defeat of Odo's rebellion in the reign of William II saw the forfeiture of all his lands that had been reinstated and four of the five dens were transferred to the Bishop of Robertsbridge. The fifth, Lindhrycg, passed to Robert de Crevecoeur, who received the Barony of Leeds Castle and whose family over the next 30 years encroached on the other dens, particularly Curtehope (1).

Over the next 300 years the church continued to wrest back most of the land it had lost prior to 1066, until Henry VIII took it all back again upon the Reformation.

INDIVIDUAL DENS

Lindhrycg and East Lindhrycg

Lindridge is the oldest recorded 'den' of Lamberhurst, dating back to 747 and owned by the Bishop of Rochester.
It was located north of the drovers' road, now the A21, and west of Cuckoo Lane.
A land charter dated between 942 and 946 attached a new pasture to Bishop Buiric's Manor at Malling (2). This was East Lindhrycg, stretching from Hoathly 'den' in the west to the boundary of the future 'Church Glebe' to the east. Its southern boundary was Parsonage Lane; its centre was Owl House.
The combined holding was the only Lamberhurst swine pasture located in Kent.
Surprisingly, it was not, however, recorded in the Domesday Book.
Lindridge Farm now occupies part of this site.

Hansfleote (an enclosure, on or near a stream)/Lamberhurst

Hansfleote was located on the north side of the river, south of the church.
Originally a swine pasture, its advantage of being located next to the River Teise and consisting of gently sloping land resulted in it being converted into a Water Meadow prior to 998 (please refer to Lamberhurst Industries, Water Meadows, for more detail).
Cited in the Domesday Book of 1086.
Hansfleote was absorbed into 'the estate of Lamberhurst' held by de Crevecoeurs in 1119, which then consisted of the den of Lamberhurst (established in 1066) and the original 'Dens' of Lindhrycg and East Lindhrycg (3).
The western side of Hansfleote, north of the river and east of the road, was renamed the Great Den of Lamberhurst by 1241 (4).
This was further sub-divided by 1568 into the Great Dens and Little Dens (5). This Survey of Lamberhurst cites 'one parcel of ground called Hanslake just east of Court Lodge'.

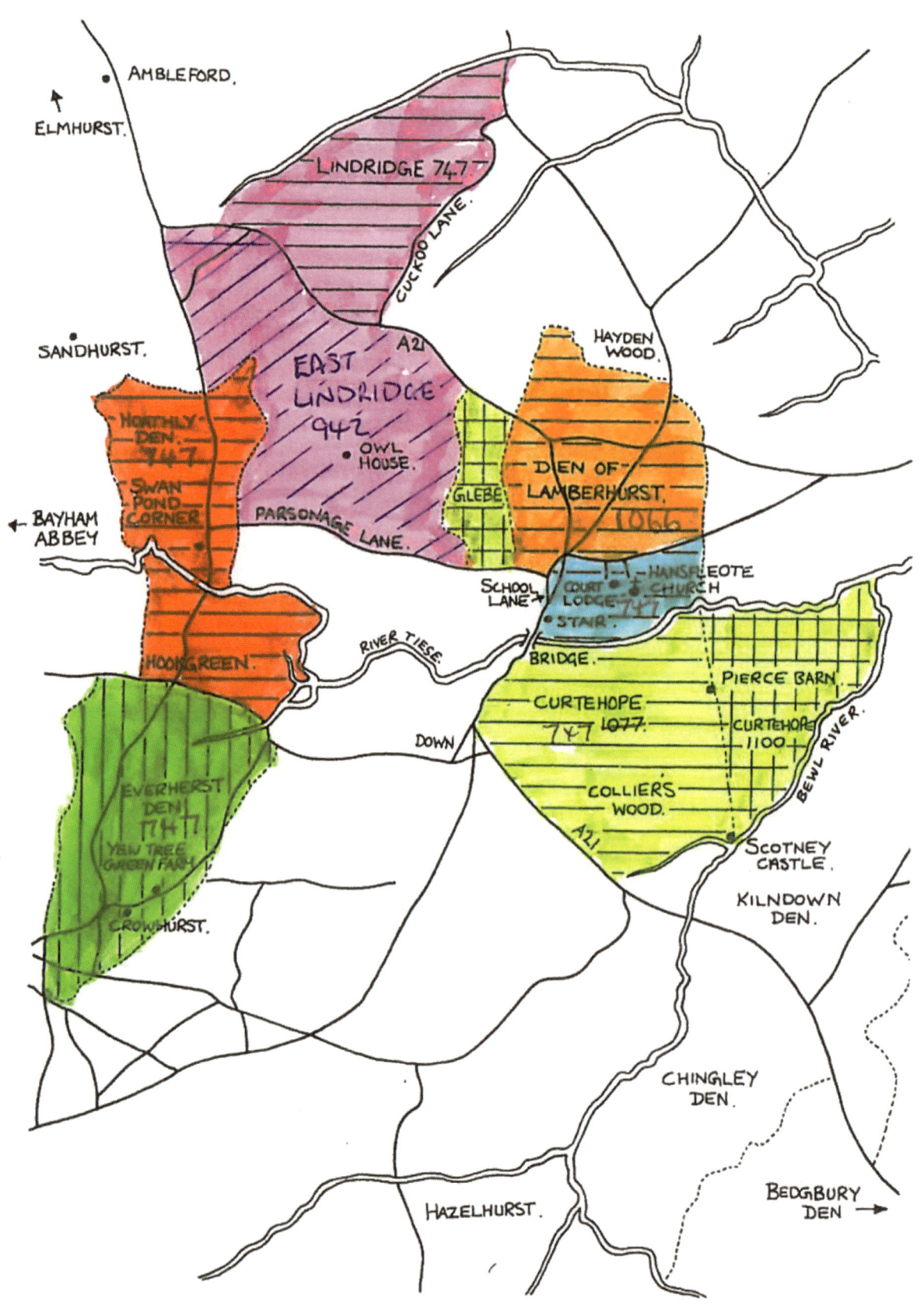

MAP OF THE LAMBERHURST DENS *CIRCA* 1200 [1]

Curtehope (an enclosure in marshland)

First cited in 1077 as being 'south of the River Teise' (4) and again in the Domesday book of 1086; its western boundary was originally The Broadway.

In 1090, the de Crevecoeurs, new Lords of the Manor of Lamberhurst, held a small portion of the land in the centre of the village named Tuttyshams. Over the next one hundred years they enlarged this area by gradually but systematically encroaching upon the den of Curtehope, pushing its western boundary to the feeder stream flowing into the River Teise east of East Mill.

However, it regained land on its eastern boundary in 1100, when the area around Pierce Barn was added and then again in 1119 with the addition of Church Glebe (now known as the Priory).

By 1171 it had been converted to a manor, the Manor of Ulcome, owned by the Archbishop of Canterbury (6) and was the nucleus of the rented Manor of Scotney by then.

On his return from the Third Crusade, William de Coliere, alias de Scotney, granted the land in free arms to the Abbey of Robertsbridge (free arms was a tax dodge to evade future knight service. The donor ran any holding given as if was still his, the recipient happy with a one-off or annual payment of goods or peppercorn. This was changed to money payment by the 1220s.)

In 1240, William de Coliere (de Scotney) is cited as holding the 'Curtinghope' of the Abbot of Robertsbridge (7).

The de Scotneys lost all their lands and manors to the Crown in 1259 after siding with the wrong side in the Second Barons War.

By 1260, the Crown had given most of the former de Scotney land to Peter de Savoy, a relative of Boniface, Archbishop of Canterbury.

The Archbishop of Canterbury's Custumal (record) of his holdings at South Malling, Sussex, of 1285 states that Peter de Savoy held Curtehope in free arms by Robertsbridge Abbey (7).

Hoathly

From very early on, Hoathly, both up and down stream, was used as a water meadow, with additional valley-bottom pasture being created by forest clearance. This site, along with Hansfleote, was the only water meadows recorded within the entire High Weald.

From around 1000, Hoathly and Crowhurst were held by the Archbishop of Canterbury's Sussex Manor of Malling, near Lewes, and the sitting tenants were the Kent Lathe of Hollingbourne (6).

Cited in the Domesday book of 1086.

In 1189, Richard I confirmed a grant of land called 'Hothlege' to Robertsbridge Abbey.

The de Scotneys were tenants and their most important holdings in the area during the first half of the 13th century were Curtehope, Hoathly and Crowhurst. They held the Manor of Hazelhust, Ticehurst, sub-vassals of the Count of Eu of Hastings, but lost it to the Crown in 1259.

In 1260, the Abbot of Robertsbridge was recorded as sole owner, so the Crown had split the land of the de Scotneys and sold to two different buyers.

The abbots used this opportunity to run the manor as they wished. They split it up into separate holdings, which resulted in an influx of well-off yeoman families from outside the parish. They in turn sub-let these units to 'hands-on tenants', who in turn sub-let to sons or overseers.

Listed as the 'Borgha [or tithing] de Hothleg' in the 1350s, it was therefore regarded as a 'reputed' manor.

Hoathly was converted to a manor by the Abbot of Robertsbridge in 1377 and became part of the Hundred of Brenchley and Horsmonden, within the Kent Lathe of Aylesford and part of the parish of Lamberhurst.

A record of 'Hodlegh' tenant rents paid to the Abbot in 1471 lists 39 separate holdings (7).

Everherste (The Outer Forest or Yew Tree Wood)

Originally the area between Yew Tree Wood and Hook Green.

The first reference to this den is when King Egbert granted a den called Ewehurst to Archbishop Wulfred, in 822 (6).

Cited in the Domesday Book of 1086, it was located south of Curtehope, between Crowhurst and Hook Green.

The Archbishop of Canterbury's Custumal (record) of 1154-1159 states that the den of 'Everherste' was held by his Manor of Ulcombe (6).

By 1285, it appears to have changed hands, as 'Euerhurst' is recorded as being held by the Abbot of Robertsbridge (7).

Amalgamated within the Manor of Lamberhurst in 1300.

Other dens were added to the original list of five.

Hayden (High Den)

Cited in 838 as den of the Primate's Manor of Snodland (6) between Lindridge and East Lindridge down to the village.

Centred around Great Cold Harbour Farm.

Bedgebury

'Begegebyra' occurs in a grant dated 814 (6).

In the Domesday Book of 1086, it was a den of Bishop Odo's Hollingbourne manor of Chart Sutton.

After Odo was stripped of all his lands in 1090, it was transferred to the de Clares of Tonbridge Castle.

PART 2 – LORDS OF THE MANOR OF LAMBERHURST AND IMPORTANT EVENTS DURING THEIR RULE

BACKGROUND

I use the title 'Lords of the Manor' generically, as it usually implies, owner of the land and ruler of the people, in which he resides.

Up to *circa* 980, there existed owners of the land which is now Lamberhurst, but no permanent occupiers, only seasonal swine drovers from Rochester.

Upon the establishment of a manor court on the site that is now occupied by Stair House, permanent occupation developed gradually. The building was used as an occasional court, in which to hear local grievances, which I am sure the 'lord' would rule on initially, to impress the local people, but the role would have been quickly delegated to his reeve to rule in his absence. Even when attending, I doubt he would have stayed, when his proper seat was a castle or an abbey. If the building was permanently occupied, it would have been by the lord's reeve.

Also, it was the general practice to let, sub-let and even sub-sub-let the land and buildings.

I do not think this situation changed until the 17th century, with the building of the third Court Lodge. However, one cannot be generalistic in this assumption; certainly there would have been times when the 'lord' did stay in Lamberhurst at 'The Halle', on the current site of Court Lodge, such as Robert de Crevecoeur, overseeing his building and colonisation programme, but I consider this would have been the exception rather than the rule.

I therefore use the title 'Lord of the Manor' as owner of the land and ruler of the people, but not a permanent resident of Lamberhurst.

AETHELBALD, KING OF MERCIA (*circa* 740-747)

AETHELBALD FEATURED ON THE REPTON SAXON STONE
Acknowledgement copyright 18/04/2010, Derby Museum and Art Gallery

At this period in time, England did not have a National King, only regional Saxon Kings who constantly conquered each others' lands. This 'King' was in fact Aethelbald, King of Mercia, who had conquered Kent. He was a Saxon warrior King who, as well as controlling Mercia (East Midlands) and Shropshire, took over Kent after defeating Aethelbert II *circa* 740.

He is depicted in the illustration above, which is from one of the two faces of the Repton Stone, the upper part of high cross that stood outside the first abbey church at Repton in Derbyshire.

He is shown riding a horse and holding a round shield, with long hair and a moustache (not visible now, but was when first discovered in 1978), armed with a sword and dressed in plate-mail armour on the upper part of his body, dated from the first half of the 8th century (84).

He was murdered by one of his own bodyguards in 757, after conquering Wessex.

The Staffordshire gold hoard discovered in 2009 in a field near Lichfield, which was the religious centre of Mercia and is perhaps the most important collection of Anglo Saxon objects ever found in England, has been dated between the years of 600 and 800 and, it has been speculated, could have been Aethelbald's.

THE BISHOPS OF ROCHESTER (*circa* 747-1066)

For over two hundred years, the area now known as the village of Lamberhurst was held by the Bishops of Rochester. During the majority of this period, the area was dense forest and was used for the fattening of swine during the pannage season, on clearings or swine pastures made in the High Wealden Forest, with only seasonal, not permanent inhabitants.

REMAINS OF THE GREAT HALL OF THE BISHOP OF ROCHESTER'S
PALACE, HIS OFFICIAL SEAT 2010

The establishment of the first village of Lamberhurst was a calculated, deliberate action by Godwin II, Bishop of Rochester, in the 990s.

Concerned at the illegal use of his swine pastures, he colonised the valley bottom with families from his Rochester lands and, to stabilise and support them, built the first wooden church of Lamberhurst, on the site of the present church, in 998, and also built a timber 'hus' (house) on the current site of Stair House, probably at the same time, for himself when in Lamberhurst, or for his representative.

BISHOP ODO OF BAYEUX (1066-1090)

Rewarded by his half-brother, William I, for being heavily involved in the planning and execution of the invasion of England, providing one hundred ships for the invasion fleet and fighting with him at the Battle of Hastings. After the battle, he was made the Earl of Kent and is listed in the Domesday Book (1086) as Bishop of Leeds, residing at Leeds Castle, formerly the Saxon Manor of Esledes. His land-holdings covered vast areas of south and east England. The only person holding more land than Odo was the king himself.

ODO (CENTRE) RALLYING THE NORMAN TROOPS AT THE BATTLE OF HASTINGS. SCENE FROM THE BAYEUX TAPESTRY WHICH HE COMMISSIONED AND WHICH WAS COMPLETED IN 1077 (8)

His main residences were listed as Dover, Rochester, Deddington (Oxfordshire) and Snettisham (Norfolk). Most of his lands in Kent were previously owned by the Bishop of Rochester. He usurped (took by force) from the church all the swine pastures around Lamberhurst.
He let the four southern swine pastures to Robert Count Eu of Hastings Castle (the Conqueror's cousin), who sub-let to the de Scotneys, lords of the manor of Hazelhurst, who had also acquired the church of Lamberhurst. Eu directly instigated William the Conqueror's wish to accelerate the colonisation of the Rape of Hastings, which ended south-west of Lamberhurst, and also his own dens adjoining it. Revolutionary for the age, he split up the huge and sprawling Saxon estates into smaller manors held on lease by his loyal Normandy knights, who were colonised with the attraction of cheap smallholding rents and zero tax.
Early clearing of the Wealden Forest was impeded by the lack of protection of the early pioneer farmers. These colonisation actions by the Normans rectified that and gave the opportunity of opening up the Weald at last. The process of clearing was not quick, but gradual, particularly in the High Weald, due to poor communication routes and the lack of transport; but a start had been made (28). Odo replaced the timber church and 'hus' with stone buildings in 1070.
He quarrelled with the king in 1082 and was imprisoned for life in Rouen and was only released by William I

immediately prior to the latter's death. However, the appointment of William's second son, William, instead of his eldest son Robert of Normandy, did not please Odo, and the year after the new king's coronation in 1087, he led a rebellion against him. He was besieged first at Pevensey Castle and then at his base at Rochester Castle and was exiled for life in France (8).

ROBERT DE CREVECOEUR – Braveheart (*circa* 1090-1155)

Hamo de Crevecoeur fought at the Battle of Hastings for William I and was rewarded by being made High Sheriff of Kent and Baron of Chatham (9).

Hamo and his family supported William II in 1088/9 in overthrowing the rebellion led by his uncle, Odo. Hamo's nephew, Robert, received the Baronetcy of Leeds from William in 1090 as thanks; this included the estate of Lamberhurst, part of Curtehope and an area in the centre of the present village, later known as Tuttysham.

LEEDS CASTLE THAT WAS THE CASTLE SEAT OF ROBERT DE CREVECOEUR 2010

He founded Leeds Abbey and Leeds Priory in 1119 (10) and made Leeds Castle his Seat of Kent in 1100 and built the walls and the vaulted cellar and also supervised great building works at Dover Castle (10).

Robert de Crevecoeur continued the colonisation strategy pioneered by Bishop Eu and supervised the building of the first mill, East Mill on Great Brooms Island, in the 1090s and the second, West Mill, on the site at Mill Bay in the early 12th century, both of which were 'grist' mills to grind corn, and he personally drove forward the establishment of the first village industries of not only milling, but also brewing and baking.

With this work, he established himself as the first proper Lord of the Manor of Lamberhurst.

He died in 1155 and was probably buried at Leeds Priory.

DANIEL DE CREVECOEUR (*circa* 1155-1210)

Robert's son and an unremarkable character, with no major achievements or happenings recorded during his tenure.

The manor was rented from Robert by Nicholas de Kenith (de Kent), in the reign of John (1199-1216), who gave the manor to the Abbot of Robertsbridge.

Daniel was buried at Leeds Priory and left the strange bequest to be remembered by a good dinner 'to the end that the Canons of that House [Leeds Priory] should have the better Commons on the day of his Orbit' (3).

HAMO DE CREVECOEUR (*circa* 1210-1266)

Daniel's grandson, Hamo, succeeded him, married the famous heiress of Folkestone, Maud de Avranches, and had a son and four daughters.

During Hamo's tenure as Lord of the Manor, he orchestrated the arrival of the second wave of colonists in the first half of the 13th century through which the process of the clearing of the High Weald forest continued. These colonists were also responsible for the dramatic success of clearing the forest that was witnessed in the Archbishop's Manor of South Malling, which included the Everherste den of Lamberhurst. This second wave were 'assarters' (essater = 'to grub up trees') who dug and ground out the smaller trees with back-breaking effort and ring-barked the larger trees for chopping down two or three years later, digging the stumps out by hand, as previous burning attempts proved useless. These people were true pioneers, adding cottages to the previously established hamlet, attending church and laying the foundations of what was to become the classic village of today's High Weald (28). (These farmer artisans and their descendants were the key to the industrial development of Lamberhurst over the next four hundred years, by supplementing their living off the land, by work in the local cloth, leather and iron industries.)

His son died before him, so Hamo confirmed the gift of the manor to the Abbot of Robertsbridge (7).

THE ARCHBISHOPS OF CANTERBURY AND THE ABBOTS OF ROBERTSBRIDGE (*circa* 1266-1540)

This decision re-kindled what was to be almost three hundred years of continuous monastic rivalry and constant litigation between the Archbishops of Canterbury and the Bishops of Robertsbridge.

Both claimed they owned the land prior to the Norman Conquest, which witnessed the constant changing of the ownership of the title Lord of the Manor of Lamberhurst, between the two parties.

There is a record of a dispute between Laurence de St Martin, Abbot of Robertsbridge, and the Boniface of Savoy, Archbishop of Canterbury, that was finally settled by Henry III in 1266.

Then a dispute was raised by Abbot Thomas with Edward I over ownership in 1293, which probably resulted from the refusal of Robert Winchelsey, Archbishop of Canterbury, to pay taxes to the king without the Pope's permission (6).

THE RUINS OF ROBERTSBRIDGE ABBEY 2010

In 1313, King Edward II appointed Walter Reynolds as Archbishop of Canterbury. Walter was a great favourite of Edward. He had been appointed the governor of Edward by his father, Edward I, and upon the new king's accession, was made a Prebendary of St Paul's, Treasurer of the Exchequer and Bishop of Worcester. In 1310, he was appointed Chancellor. Upon the death of Gaveston, Archbishop of Canterbury, and at the insistence of the king, Walter was made Archbishop, overruling the monks' election of Thomas Cobham, Dean of Salisbury. The position of chancellor was dissolved in 1314 and the responsibilities taken over by the new Keeper of the Great Seal, which was Walter himself. He was now the second most important man in England, after the king (11, 12).

THE TOMB OF WALTER REYNOLDS IN CANTERBURY CATHEDRAL 2010

It was therefore not a surprise that on 1st June 1314, Edward II's primate granted the Archbishop the right to hold a weekly market (on what is now The Broadway) and a fair (on Fair Field, which is behind the current Chequers Oast), in Lamberhurst.

The income from ownership of the land was phenomenal. Not only was it generating rental income, but also raised 'tithe'. Tithe was the income accrued as a 'tax' on parishioners for the provision of a priest at Lamberhurst church to cure the souls of the parish. This was collected at one tenth of income or of the value of land leased. The ramification of this decision was the massive development in the importance of Lamberhurst in the High Weald over the next two hundred years.

HENRY VIII (1540-1542)

Dissolved the abbeys and took over the manor in 1540.

THE SIDNEY FAMILY (1542-1733)

Henry quickly disposed of his new assets and the Manor of Lamberhurst was sold to **Sir William** Sidney and his wife Anne in 1542.

William was the courtier to the king and tutor of his son, the future Edward VI. He was one of the commanders at the Battle of Flodden in 1513, which annihilated the Scottish threat once and for all, and was knighted for his contribution, but held the title for just 2 years (13).

SIR WILLIAM'S TOMB AT PENSHURST PLACE (13)

SIR HENRY 1573 (13)

His son **Sir Henry** took over the title upon his father's death in 1554 and became a prominent politician, courtier and soldier.

He was a close friend of Edward VI (who reputedly died in Henry's arms at Greenwich Palace in 1553) and Elizabeth I, who made him Lord President of Wales and Lord Deputy of Ireland. He commanded many victories over the Irish and Welsh and pioneered the first deliberate attempt to colonise Ireland.

He lived most of his life in Ireland and Wales, but importantly was responsible for ordering the great Lamberhurst Manor Survey of 1568.

Died at Ludlow Castle in 1586 (13).

Sir Robert, his second son, inherited the manor on Henry's death.

Statesman, poet and a patron of the arts, he was created Baron Sidney of Penshurst, Viscount De L'Isle and 1st Earl of Leicester by James I.

Like his predecessors, he spent little time in Kent. He was member of Parliament for Glamorgan, fought in

Holland with his elder brother Philip and with his uncle against Spain.

Sir Philip, his elder brother, was mortally wounded at the Battle of Zutphen in Holland in 1586, which is why Robert, not Philip, succeeded his father.

Robert sold the manor to John Porter Esq in 1603, the 3rd year of Charles 1, in order to finance his semi-private expeditions in Ireland.

Robert Sidney died in 1606 (13).

There is no record of the Sidneys ever living in Lamberhurst (4).

SIR HENRY LEAVING DUBLIN CASTLE (14)

SIR ROBERT (13)

Michael Zell, in his book *Early Modern Kent*, gives an excellent picture of what an average farm in Lamberhurst was like under the Sidneys, 1540-1640: 'most of the land was still held by a limited number of frequently absent landowners, which afforded considerable flexibility to their tenant farmers. The leased farms were small, 41% under five acres and 38% between five and fifty acres.

Equal prominence was given to oats and wheat. Nearly all had cattle, on average thirteen in the early 1600s. Oxen were the main field work animal, not horses. The average Lamberhurst farmer during this period was a self-sufficient mixed farmer, still set apart from the outside world. He would split his land into plough and pasture areas and apply strict rotational use. His timetable would have been oats or wheat in year one, peas in year two, a repeat of year one for year three, then six years of clover lay for fattening cattle and sheep.' This cycle of plough and pasture was vital to protect the soil.

THE PORTER FAMILY (1603-1733)

The Porter family was an old established family based at Begeham (Bayham), who originated from Markham in Nottinghamshire (83).

John Porter, third generation, rebuilt and lived at Court Lodge from 1634 (10, 50). He leased 100 acres of land on the south bank of the River Teise, below the church, to William Darell of Scotney Castle, with the right 'to make weirs and floodgates in the river to flood the meadows' (1). I do not think this ever happened.

Some sources indicate that the Sidneys maintained ownership of the manor. I view this now as not to be the case, as in 1733 it was purchased outright from Elizabeth Chapman, the great grand-daughter of John Porter (10).

THE MORLAND FAMILY (1733-1934)

William Morland of Westmorland purchased the manor from the said Elizabeth Chapman.

After 1700 years, Lamberhurst finally witnessed its first Lord of the Manor who actually had a residential seat in the village.

The Morlands were known throughout history as substantial landowners in north-west England.

Also, William's father-in-law founded Liverpool and was in charge of a large business importing Virginian tobacco to the port.

He enlarged his estate by purchasing farms in Lamberhurst.

He died in 1774 and was buried in Lamberhurst church (15).

WILLIAM MORLAND
(Holding the deed of sale for
Court Lodge) (60)

THOMAS MORLAND (60)

His only son, **Thomas**, inherited the manor from his father in 1774, plus lands in Brenchley and Horsmonden.
Made Court Baron in 1772, he died in 1784 (15).

It then appears that there were no direct-line descendants and the manor was held in trust by the family for a **William Alexander** Morland, the closest living relative, who was 16 at the time, born at Westminster St James and presumably still living there.
In 1790, he is listed on the tax list of Lamberhurst, so must have inherited the manor at this date.
His brother, Charles, living at Canterbury, released his Lamberhurst lands to William about the same time.
William undertook a massive increase in his estate. In his marriage settlement, he gained a farm in Wadhurst, one in Playden and three in Brenchley. He then proceeded to purchase farms in and around Lamberhurst: Calves Acre (actually 5, which he added to his park); Hoghole, Owls Castle, Dungate farms; Windmill lands and Cutthorn.
He records in 1820, 'I am the only male person bearing the name of Morland now left in this part of the globe' (15).
Died at Court Lodge in 1847, presumably with no children.
He left a bequest of £200 in his will to the village school (15).

William Courtney was born in Westminster St James in 1818 and inherited the manor on the death of his uncle, William Alexander, in 1847.
WCM became a legend and kept a diary, which is my main source of information here.

WILLIAM ALEXANDER (60)   WILLIAM COURTNEY left (60)

He was the archetypal Victorian squire, hard but compassionate to his farm tenants and who took a modern approach to land management, always willing to try out new ideas and to experiment with new breeds in animal husbandry.

WCM continued the expansion by his uncle by purchasing local smallholdings and lands, mainly woodland, held by absentee landlords, plus property. Indeed, there appears to have been only one yeoman (who owned the land he farmed), a Richard Springett, as the tenant farmers did not have the money to buy their farms. Recorded on the web site of the Morland family as purchasing: Tile House, seven cottages, Spray Hill Cottage and two cottages on The Down, all in Lamberhurst; Crouch fields, half an acre of The Down, Cold Harbour and Lamberhurst Forge and land of Packs Pasture in Lamberhurst.

In his early years, staff are recorded as living at Court Lodge. The 1881 Census lists WCM and his wife, plus a coachman, a lady's maid, a cook, two housemaids, a kitchen maid and a house boy. At the Keepers Cottage a gamekeeper and his family, at the Gardeners Cottage a gardener and his family. Altogether there were twenty-one people living on the estate.

Over the next two censuses only WCM and his wife are listed as living there, but as he was then in his 70s and 80s that is hardly surprising.

He took no nonsense from his tenant farmers, evicting them if they did not comply with his rules and standards, but he was also very generous, repairing buildings, draining fields and supporting them through years of serious loss of cattle due to disease between 1865 and 1873 and the depression in the markets during the 1870s, when the American prairies were opened up, which had a devastating effect on the English corn market due to economies of scale.

He personally visited all his farms once a month.

He farmed his own estate, which was multi-functional.

In animal husbandry he majored on cattle. His main breeds were Sussex and Shorthorns, although he experimented with Ayrshire, Shetland, Alderney and Brittany. These were raised for beef, but were also bred for sale, as recorded in 1866, when he sold twenty-five Shorthorns for £610 and thirty-one other cattle for £435. Even their dung was sold to hop farmers.

He must also have had a dairy herd, as in 1864 he records a dairy at Court Lodge; but, ironically, he refused to let his tenant farmers change over from beef to dairy cattle.

He kept a herd of sheep for wool and again bred for sale, selling seventy-five for £134 in 1866.

He records in his diary that, in 1877, twenty of his lambs were killed by lightning.

Crops grown on his own and tenant farmer lands are recorded as beans, hay, oats, apples, turnips, mangolds, clover and potatoes.

In 1856, he purchased a steam engine with threshing gear and a steam plough, after seeing one at work at the Canterbury Show.

He even experimented with railways: in 1864, he 'looked at laying down of a new Boydell's self-acting railway', which probably ran from Pullens Farm to Court Lodge.

Lamberhurst Manor had its own woodworking shop, on the site of the present Timber Yard Cottage on Church Lane, where he installed a vertical saw in the timber yard and also had its own workforce of building workers.

He took an active role in village matters, particularly the school and the church. He was a trustee of the former, gave £200 for the building of a second storey and the clock tower (the initials WAM are carved on the south-east gable) and attended the latter twice every Sunday.

He organised social events for his workforce: weekday cricket matches on Court Lodge Park in summer, where his workers were given the whole day off to play or to watch; a 'Workman's Treat' every January and a 'Servants Ball' every December (16).

He died at Court Lodge in 1909, at the astounding age of 91; the whole of the village must have mourned.

Colonel Henry Morland
Son of William Courtney. Born 1855.

COLONEL HENRY (60)   THE MORLAND FAMILY CREST 2010

Inherited the manor from his father in 1909.

Gained the rank of Colonel in the services of the 9th Lancers, and travelled to India and Morocco.

He built the first golf course, 9-hole only, at Lamberhurst, on his father's parkland, in 1890. It was a club for the local gentry, with membership limited to 50. Poet Siegfried Sassoon, who was a regular player, commented that 'it was maintained by sheep'.

It was leased to a group of local businessmen in 1923, who redesigned it.

Married twice to daughters of gentry. In 1884, he married Lady Alice Maud Neville (whose father was Sir William Neville, 1st Marquis of Abergavenny, who lived at Eridge Castle) at Frant Church. Unfortunately, his wife died young. In 1902, he married Bessie Josephine Laird, daughter of John Laird, the Birkenhead shipbuilder.

They had three children: Violet Alice 1886, William 1903 and John Courtney 1904 (the latter in Cheshire).

He died in 1934 (15).

The Manor of Lamberhurst was dissolved in 1936.

Court Lodge and its surrounding lands, including the golf course, is still owned by the descendants of William, Mr & Mrs Nicholas Morland, who live in part of Court Lodge.

A late 1900s chest tomb to the Morland family is situated in the Parish Church of Lamberhurst graveyard, ten metres west of the church. It is inscribed with the family coat of arms and carries the inscription, 'The monument of the Morland Family stands suitably between the church and the Morland's home at Court Lodge'.

PART 3 – THE MAIN ACTIVITIES AND INDUSTRIES OF LAMBERHURST

INTRODUCTION

Historically, Lamberhurst has attracted a range of activities and industry; some had starts and finishes, and some have been continuous.
What I have tried to record are its main activities and the times when they were at their peak. For instance, swine fattening no longer continues today in this area, sheep pasturing still does, but not to the extent it did in the 12th and 13th centuries.

SWINE FATTENING (*circa* 747-1100)

From the 700s, the area now known as Lamberhurst was used mainly for the fattening of Rochester drovers' swine during the pannage season. They had the right to graze pigs and sheep and to fell timber and were accorded the rights by the owner of the land, the Bishop of Rochester. They would drive their swine herds down into the forest and made clearings for swine pastures, called 'dens', made in the High Wealden forest of Caesterweraweald. For a minimum of two hundred years, they would have been the only inhabitants and seasonal, as permanent habitation of the area had not begun, as it was a dark, foreboding place, thick in upland forest and valley marshes, making all-year-round travel impossible and developing images of ghouls, dragons and demons.
The pannage season was from 25th September to 22nd November, after which the swine were driven home and slaughtered. Swine drovers would travel huge distances to legally and illegally use the swine pastures of Lamberhurst, rich in acorns (oak dominated beech on clay soils). Beech mast was the preferred feed for swine, but it could only be relied on in three or four years out of ten, whereas oak provided regular annual feed, which is why the dens of Lamberhurst were so valuable. It is very important to note that pannage contributed greatly to the development of Lamberhurst through the elimination of new forest growth and the task of forest clearing to established trees only.
'Pannage stands as a classic example of how to eliminate a forest. Simply cut off the seed supply and wait' (54).

MEDIEVAL SWINE DROVERS (12)

The combined actions of Godwin II, Bishop of Rochester, to colonise the area (see Lords of the Manor chapter) and the economic decision of the Hollingboune drovers to slaughter on site after the pannage season ended, rather than drive the swine back home to slaughter them, resulted in the establishment of the initial village of Lamberhurst.

Cattle, not swine, would have represented a better return, but as there were few open meadows in the area at this time, grazing was restricted to the floor of the forest and, although having no effect on swine, cattle eating green acorns would be poisoned.

The location of these swine pastures are detailed in the chapter The Dens of Lamberhurst.

It may be difficult to understand today, but back then this activity was very important and profitable, witnessed by over four hundred years of continuous dispute and litigation over the rights to graze swine in the High Wealden forest area, that was to become Lamberhurst.

By the 1100s, with the gradual clearing of the High Weald forest, swine pasturing began to be replaced by sheep farming as the main agrarian activity.

THE LAMBERHURST WATER MEADOWS (*circa* 940-1300)

Background

A water meadow was an area of pasture within a river valley that was deliberately 'flooded' to encourage the growth of grass used for agrarian fodder. I use the word 'flooded' in a descriptive manner, as flooding would kill the grass; the intention was not to flood the meadow, but to keep a trickle of water flowing over the grass roots and growing points of the spring growth, just enough to warm them and protect them from frosts. The water also deposited nutrients that encouraged better grass growth. This resulted in the production of early spring grass, allowing stock to be fed in early spring, when normally stored hay would be running out, and so more animals could be brought through the winter.

It was a precise and planned management of land requiring the accurate control of water depth, flow and drainage of water over a considerable acreage.

Its construction would have been to partly divert the flow of the river into a series of water-carrying channels, feed channels, drains and water stops that had been excavated across it.

The water stops or 'hatches' in Saxon times would have consisted of timber boards placed into vertically slotted stones, which, by adding or taking away boards, controlled the flow of water into and out of the water meadow and consequently its water depth. Their size would have ranged from seven-board depth from the main water source to a single-board depth the width of a spade on the channels and drains (72). Water meadow hay was inferior in quality to normal meadow hay, but it was available much earlier and in greater quantities. Although expensive to construct and maintain, water meadows increased the rental value of fields by up to four-fold.

The increased use of fertilisers on normal meadows and the significant increase in the cost of farm labour during the first half of the 20th century meant that the operation of water meadows was uneconomic and so the few remaining operations still in existence were converted to normal crop production.

Hanslake Field Water Meadows

Alongside Hoathly, Hanslake is the only known Saxon water meadow in Britain.

Although nothing remains today, it is arguably the most important structure in the entire history of Lamberhurst.

It was situated east of the Little and Great Dens on the north bank of the River Teise, directly south of the church, and was approximately fifteen acres in area.

Its southern boundary was the River Teise, its western boundary the Lady Well stream (current eastern boundary hedge of the golf course), its eastern boundary the feeder stream that runs down the side of the Lamberhurst bypass and its northern boundary a banking of earth that is still visible in the field, but which was originally much higher and probably the remains of terracing from strip farming and was the route of the old Cranbrook

Road of 900 that connected the Archbishop's lands in Sussex and West Kent.

The importance of the Lamberhurst water meadows is historically documented for over three hundred years of almost constant arguing of ownership from 998 to 1300s. From this earliest date, Godwin 1st, the Bishop of Rochester, recorded that he was very concerned about the possible loss of ownership of his Hansfleote (an enclosure in or near a stream) water meadow (2). It is referenced in 1077 as 'Hansfleote, the managed water meadow below the church' (34). By 1568, it is recorded as 'Hanslake field' (5). The subsequent suffix 'Meade' for this site, 'Lady Meade' and 'Lady Meade field', indicates this was part of the flood plain of the River Teise.

LOOKING NORTH FROM THE RIVER TEISE 2010

Hanslake is unique. It did not employ the traditional method of using the River Teise as its source of water, but the spring of Lady Well on its north-west edge, using the river only as its outflow.

The last reference of any trace of the water meadow was in the 1970s: 'one lock was situated so as to block the flow from the stream, another where the feed-sewer entered the river. A third controlled the flow from the Lady Well. A metal sluice gate, once covered by thick undergrowth under the hedge row (on its western boundary below Lady Well), has finally rusted away' (1). The latter reference would probably have been to a metal rack and pinion system that raised and lowered the wooden gate mechanically, that replaced the original manual timber-board system. It would have been manufactured in a local foundry, which would have had traditionally provided the machinery for use in watermills (72).

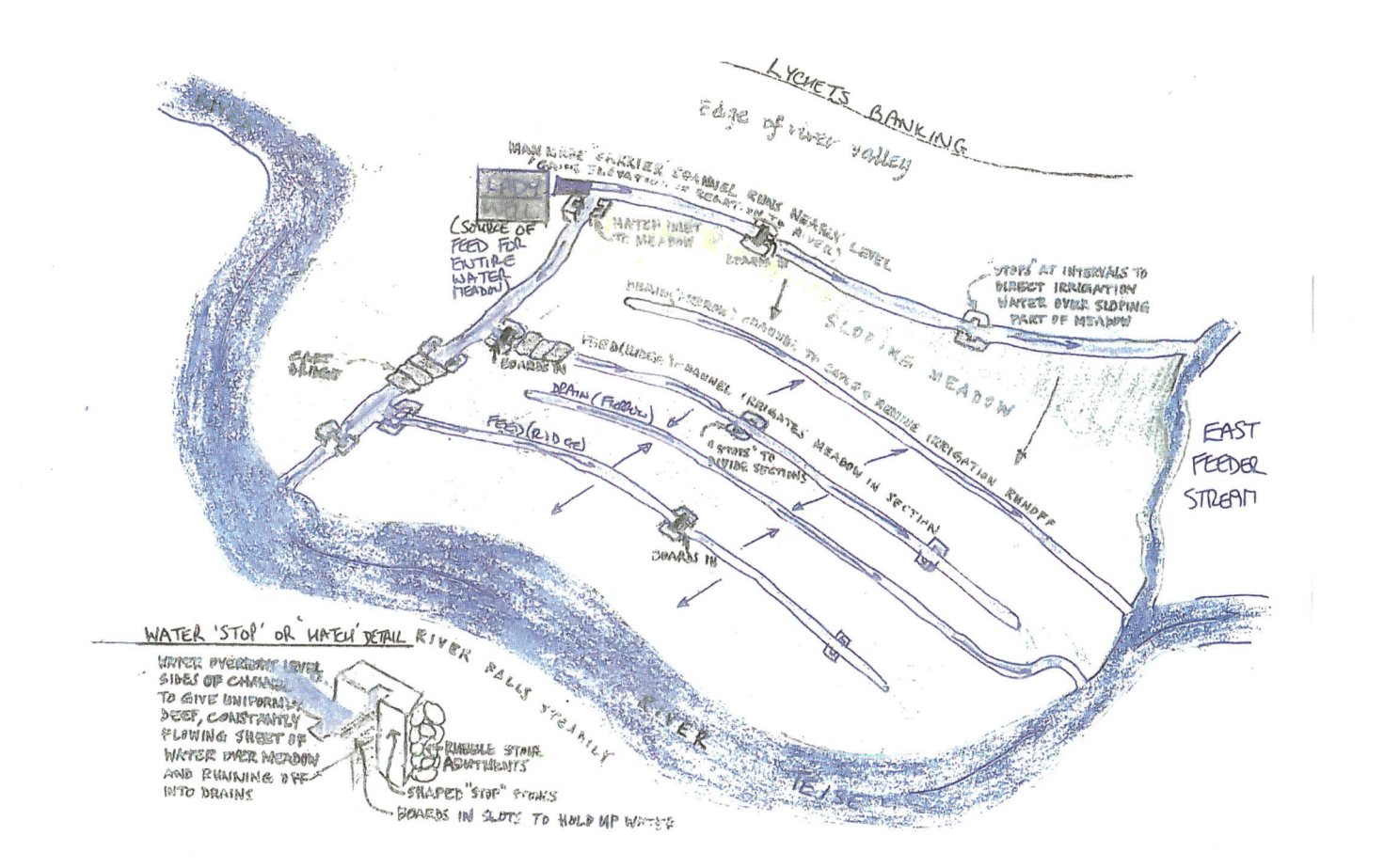

ARTIST'S IMPRESSION

Unfortunately, no trace of the water meadow now remains visible, although I suspect that remains of the water stop stones still lie buried beneath the ground.

WOOL (*circa* 940-1280)

Sheep rearing for the sale of wool began slowly around 940 in this area and would have developed to be the first recognised 'industry' of the village.
'Lamberhurste' was recorded in 1115 (17), which one interpretation translates as 'wooded hill for lambs or lambing, near a stream'. Around this date, therefore, we are certain that the raising of sheep for the export of wool was replacing swine fattening as the main source of employment and also provided a considerable surplus of moveable wealth.
Lamberhurst was one of only a few sites suitable for the raising and grazing of sheep outside Romney Marsh. The valley bottom and the immediate slopes, especially south of the River Teise, up towards the present Pierce Barn area as well as The Down, were ideal for the raising of sheep. The river valley at Hoathly was also particularly fertile and important.
At the time of shearing, farmers would have herded the sheep into collecting pens in the valley bottom and dammed the River Teise to create a small pond, which was called a 'wash fold'. They would have then lowered the sheep into the water and allowed them to swim round for several minutes. Farmers would have stood up to their waists in the water to duck the sheep several times to make sure they were completely soaked. The swimming action caused the wool to float, allowing the water to penetrate to the skin and wash out all unwanted dirt and excess grease. This made the wool easier to clip and reduced its weight for transporting. It was then dried and baled.

SHEEP GRAZING, LAMBERHURST 2010

By the 1200s, English land was cheap, but labour was scarce, so the economy of England was based on raw production, not manufacture. For this reason, the production of raw wool was centred in England, but the manufacture of wool cloth was centred in Western Europe. Raw wool was shipped to the textile cities of Flanders, notably Ypres and Ghent. In the 1200s, only 10% of wool production was used for domestic textile manufacture.

Wool was a great source of income for the Crown, which from 1275 imposed an export tax on wool, called the 'Great Custom'. Avoidance of the tax by smuggling, known as 'owling', was severely dealt with, punishable by the cutting off of a hand. In extreme cases, particularly if the offence included violent conduct, the punishment was even more extreme, as recorded in 1748/9, when a member of the infamous Hawkhurst Gang, living on The Slade in Lamberhurst, was caught, convicted and then hanged, drawn and quartered.

Owl House, Little Owl House, Owlcastle Wood and Owls Castle Farm may identify the smuggling route southwards out of the parish, to the channel coast. (The smugglers used coded hoot calls to avoid tax officers, hence the term 'owling'.)

The importance of the production of wool to the economy at that time can be shown by the fact that the presiding officer of the House of Lords sat on the 'wool sack', a chair stuffed with wool.

WOOL

However, by the 1280s, the export of raw wool market was virtually wiped out as a result of the fall in the price of wool, the loss of overseas markets by the development of raw wool production in Europe and a virulent sheep disease. From this time, cattle predominantly replaced sheep as the main agrarian activity in the area (50). However, sheep continued to be kept, although not on such a grand scale, as it was recorded as late as 1909 that the Lamberhurst shepherds continued to be 'recognised with much respect' (52).

BAKING (*circa* 950-Present)

The baking industry ran hand in hand with the cider-brewing industry and began in late Saxon times.
Robert de Crevecoeur's decision to build his water-driven East Mill and West Mill, in the late 11th and early 12th centuries had a massive effect on the population of Lamberhurst (3).
Up until then, the villagers had to grind grain by hand in a pestle and mortar to produce flour, made into a rough mash by adding water and baked over open fires, to produce a coarse type of bread (18).
The ability of the water-driven mills to grind corn and produce a finer flour in far greater quantities substantially reduced the time and effort it took to bake bread and produced a higher quality staple food for the average villager, in greater quantities.
This would not have been the light white loaf that we know today; it would have been dark bread made from barley, millet and other coarse grains made into bran loaves, but was a massive improvement (18, 19).
In 1138, Helyas de Crevecoeur, Lord of the Manor, in his grant to Leeds Priory, cites his 'mills, ovens and orchards in Lamberhurst'. Two bakeries are listed, one on the current Chequers Inn site, the other on the land to the rear of 'the wic' site, currently occupied by Stair House.
'Maurice the Baker' is cited in the grant, so he is the first named baker in the village (3).
The 'wic' site bakery was transferred to Combwell Priory in 1172, by Emma de Crevecoeur (4); the named baker on the site was Elias Pistor.
In the early medieval times, with a rising population, other bakers would have started appearing, enabling villages to choose instantly what type and what quality of bread they wanted without the effort of baking at

home.

Bakers Guilds were established to regulate the industry by placing controls on price and quality of the bread and in 1202 the first laws were introduced to control it. Any baker breaking the law could be pilloried, fined and even banned from baking for life (18).

A letter in 1240 from the Prior of Combwell to the Abbot of Robertsbridge asks for witnesses for a new lease of a baking and brewing workshop to the rear of Stair House.

The Chequers Inn site was granted to Leeds Priory, held by the Archbishop of Canterbury in the 1250s, who by 1284 is recorded as leasing it to a Lawrence Tavel. Hugh and Ralph the 'bakers' are cited (3).

In 1266, The Assize of Bread introduced the first bread subsidy to help make bread more affordable to the poor (19).

MEDIEVAL BREAD MAKING (19)   BREAD BAKING 2010

By the Tudor times, there had evolved three different qualities of bread, for the different socio-economic groups. The finer white loaves were a status symbol and were confined, due to its expense, to the nobility and land owners. Merchants and tradesmen could afford wheaten cobs, whilst the poor still had to make do with the bran loaves (19).

A Nicholas Gyllot, living on the north side of Brewer Street, just west of the Gill Stream (The White Swan), is cited in 1551 as 'a bread maker and brewer of ales' and was still active during the 1560s (4).

In 1840, two bakers are recorded in Lamberhurst: William Barton and Charles Osborne (21).

Three bakers are recorded in the 1881 Census: one at River Cottages, one at Pierce Cottages and a John Avard living in Millhouse, baker and confectioner, who in 1869 had opened his shop on the High Street.

AVARDS BAKERY IN 1910 (78)
(John Avard is holding the tray of bread)

In Pelham's Directory of 1901, a one S. Fullbrook is listed as baker and corn dealer in Lamberhurst. Peter Sands can remember this business occupying the bay-windowed 2 High Street, almost opposite Avards, closing in the 1970s.

Avards bakery still continues the 1000-year-old industry in the village, operating from Arnold House, which was built by the miller who owned Town Mill and Bartley Mill and bears his name. Older residents remember that there was a long history of individual households making cakes and taking them to Avards, for baking.

CORN MILLING (1090-1800)

THE EAST MILL

The first water mill in Lamberhurst was built on Great Brooms Island, on the south bank of the River Teise, due south of the parish church. Named the East Mill, it was built by Robert de Crevecoeur, Lord of the Manor of Lamberhurst, in 1090. It was called a 'grist mill', which meant it was used for the milling of corn (3).

This was very late being built, as mills were a feature of every village in England at the time. The Domesday Survey of 1086 lists 5,634, which is one for every three hundred inhabitants.

I suspect the reason for this was that the population of Lamberhurst at that time was only one hundred inhabitants.

CLASSIC DESIGN OF A NORMAN WATER-DRIVEN UNDERSHOT GIST MILL

It would have been built in the classical mill design, which was three floors and water powered.

A sluice gate would have opened a channel to start the water flowing over or under a vertically mounted water wheel.

A large gear wheel, called the 'pit wheel', would have been mounted on the same axle as the water wheel and would have driven a smaller gear-wheel, the 'wallflower', converting the horizontal power to a vertical power by being connected to the main drive-shaft. The use of gears would have increased the rotation from 10 rpm at the water wheel end to 120 rpm on the drive-shaft.

The millstones themselves were laid one on top of the other. The bottom stone, called the 'bed', was fixed to the 'stone floor', while the top stone, the 'runner', was mounted on the drive-shaft and was agitated by the 'vibrating shoe'. A wheel called a 'stone nut' and one called the 'crown wheel', mounted on the main shaft, were also connected to a running spindle, used to power other machinery, such as a wooden drum to wind up a chain used to hoist sacks of grain ready to be milled, to the 'sack floor' at the top of the mill. One or both were used in classical designs.

The process of milling was to empty the sacks of grain into 'grain bins' on the sack floor, which was channelled via a 'grain spout' into the 'grain hopper', from which it would fall into a hole in the centre of the 'runner stone' and would be crushed between the two stones. The milled grain (flour) was collected as it emerged through grooves in the 'runner stone' from its outer rim and fed down a 'meal spout' into sacks on the ground or 'meal' floor.

All the working parts, consisting of the shaft, spindles, gears and nuts, would have been manufactured locally from wood, preferably yew.

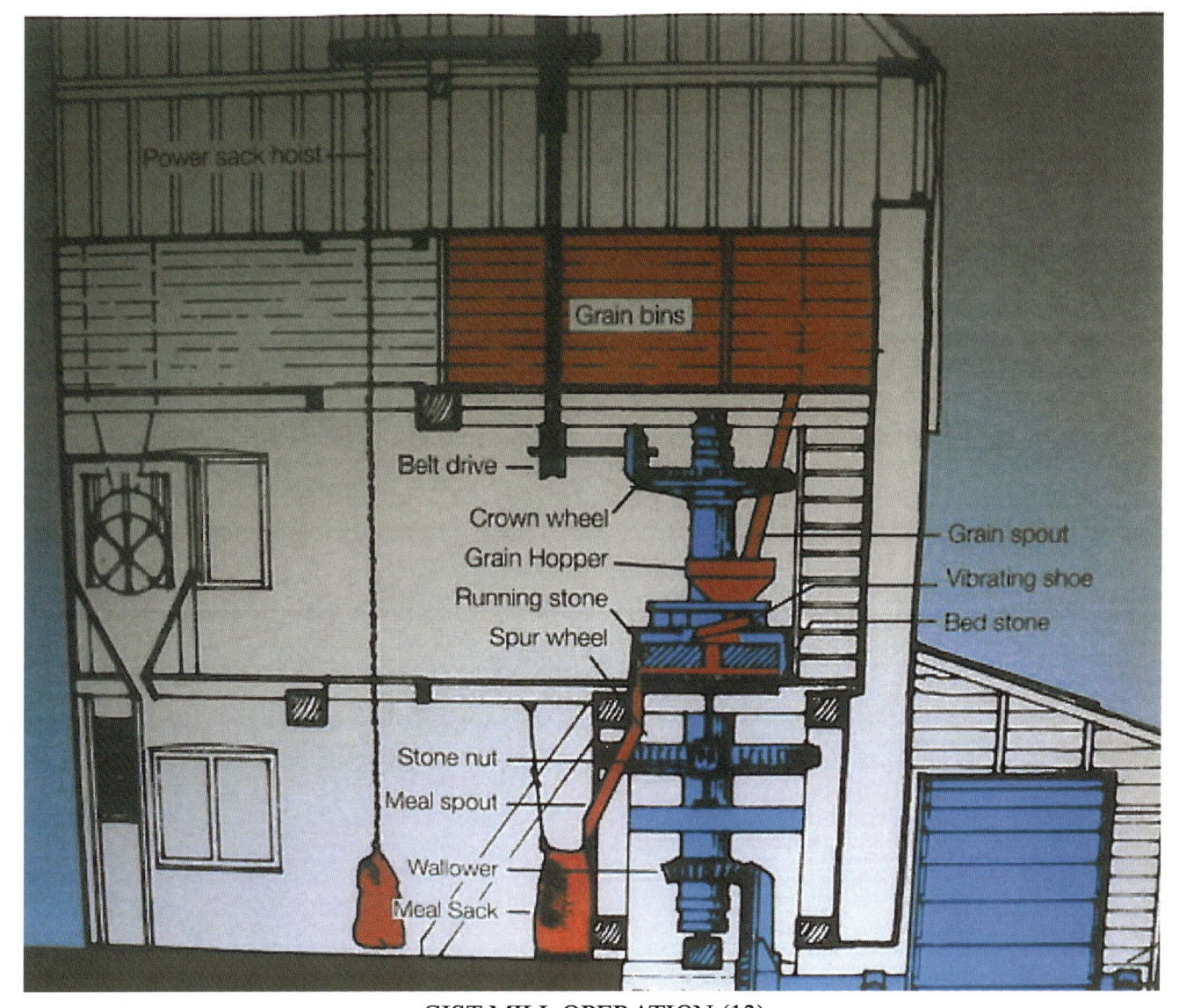

GIST MILL OPERATION (13)

The next intimation of a mill on the Great Brooms 'island' was in 1137, when Hamo de Crevecoeur, Lord of the Manor of Lamberhurst and grandson of Robert, granted all the water mills of the estate of Lamberhurst to Leeds Priory (then owned by the Archbishop of Canterbury, William de Corbell) (3).

In 1228, a feet of fines states that 'Nicholas de Kenet [de Kent] acknowledges the rent of ten shillings, to be the right of the Prior of Leeds of the mill of Lamberhurst' (3).

The de Kents sub-let the manor of Lamberhurst from the de Crevecoeurs through the estate tenant of the de Thurnhams.

After the second Barons War, which ended in 1267, Roger, the Abbot of Robertsbridge, held the Lamberhurst Manor supreme, which included East Mill.

The abbey's account rolls of the manor estate make mention of the East Mill in 1323, when the weir sluices were repaired (7).

In 1369, the abbot paid out for the 'scouring and cleaning out [of] the ditches at and around Londymede'. This took 24 days of work at a rate of 4d per day (7).

In 1371, major repair work was carried out on the water mill structure. The abbey's bursar books of the 15th century record similar repairs (7).

The East Mill appears to have ceased operation after 1500.

The Lamberhurst Manor Survey of 1568 cites, 'Great Brooms with a little island where sometime stood the

East Mill, five acres and one yard' (5). The 'dry ditch of Great Brooms Island' is cited in 1768. The Ordnance Survey Maps of 1851, 1869, 1910 and 1930 showed the oxbow loop around the island.

Up until the 1960s, the island site was a small scrub wood; it is now part of the surrounding ploughed field.

It is still just possible to discern the oxbow horseshoe indentation of the island in the field, which was the original river course.

The current course of the river is the former mill race.

Nothing is visible above ground of the East Mill today.

TOWN OR WEST MILL (LONG WALK 2)

Originally situated at Mill Bay on the River Teise, behind Mill House and Mill Cottage. It was built by Robert de Crevecoeur in the 1090s and was the second mill built in Lamberhurst. Like its predecessor, it was a 'grist mill', which was used for the milling of corn (3).

By 1228, the tenants, the de Kents, had given the mill to Robertsbridge Abbey, in free arms, as it is not listed in the Leeds Priory record above (7). The abbey's bursar books of the 15th century record two separate entries for repairs 'to the two water mills within the manor' (7).

Originally recorded as a corn grist mill in the Lamberhurst Manor Account Rolls of 1323-1327 (4). In 1422, Ralph Clerk, churchwarden of Lamberhurst Church, is recorded as 'holding the water mill at Mill Bay' (4).

The will of a Thomas Relfe, in 1475, recorded that he had left the water mill to his wife Agnes.

WEST/TOWN MILL 1860 (78)

In 1487, Nicholas Fowle, a member of the Frant family of iron masters, acquired the mill, along with Mill House, from Thomas May of Wadhurst and John Remys of Lamberhurst, 'powered by a water wheel' (1).

The will of John Fowle (son of Nicholas), in 1519, left the mill to his widow and his son Richard.

The Survey of the Manor of Lamberhurst of 1568 states that the heirs of John Barham held "one water mill and one garden called Taint Garden'.

In 1618, John's son Robert died, owning the property.

By 1840, it was owned by Elizabeth Barton, who leased it to one John Jones (1).

In the 1881 Census, a Miller's Grinder is recorded as living at River Cottages (also known as Waterlane Cottages). In 1886, Elizabeth sold the mill to Thomas Parker of Ridge Farm (1).

WEST/TOWN MILL AND SLUICE GATE
(Mill on extreme left) 1905 (78)

As we have seen, the East Mill closed in the 1500s, but the West Mill was still in constant use, milling grain up to the late 1800s, when the introduction of roller milling revolutionised the industry by producing higher quality white flour rather than wholemeal flour that the grist mills produced, and was the death knell for them within a generation. It was last used for milling corn in 1914.

In the 1920s, a Colonel Delamain, who lived at 'The Brook' (now Murlingden), purchased the land known as 'Palmers Croft', which consisted of the mill and Murlingden, from Colonel Sir Henry Morland, the last Lord of the Manor of Lamberhurst. He converted the mill to produce an intermittent supply of electricity to the village (he is also recorded as a part-owner of Lamberhurst Motor Company Ltd on the present Ricarde's Flats site). The supply was direct current and was only used as lighting, as there was no means of storage.

In 1924, a generator was purchased to replace water as a power source, as its main source (the mill wheel) was still used whenever the water flow was adequate, but constantly broke down. Therefore, a Mr Nichols, an 'outside expert', was brought in and practically lived on-site. He trained up a local man as his replacement, a Victor Corbett, who lived at 3 Slade Cottages.

Much of the village nucleus was connected up to this supply. No meters were installed: Delamain employed 'collectors' as a fixed weekly charge was levied after installation and consumption was estimated (1).

Listed in Kelly's *Directory of Kent* as 'Lamberhurst Electric Supply, Power Station, Town Mill'.

A succession of court actions by farmers, whose land bordering the River Teise was constantly flooded, brought Delamain to the brink of bankruptcy (one instance in 1926 was when Delamain raised the sluice when the river was flowing slow, which then stuck).

A Mr Halsey of The Mount provided capital to sustain the operation until 1933, with the arrival of mains supply (1).

Demolished in 1953, little trace of the building survives, but evidence of the sluice gates and channels can be viewed from the footbridge over the river.

THE TOWN WINDMILL

Grade II Listed building; former site of the windmill that took advantage of the easterly winds that blew down the River Teise valley powered the woodworking machinery for Edward Padgham, who had the largest

carpentry business in the village, employing 4 men (it was never used for milling corn).
It is situated on the south side of the High Street at the bottom, behind the Parish Offices.

THE TOWN WINDMILL 1860 (78)

Three-storey timber-framed building built in the late 1800s, with one two-storey extension and one single-storey extension; weatherboarded on a brick base and corrugated iron roof.
Two loft doors on first floor with outline of removed gable extension.
Destroyed by fire after being struck by lightning in 1897. An eyewitness account said, 'it looked like a giant Catherine Wheel'.
Converted to residential use in 2005.

THE TOWN WINDMILL SITE 2010

HOATHLY OR FURNACE MILL
Grade II Listed Mill; wall and outbuildings originally built in the 1700s and extended early 1800s. Timber-framed structure, weatherboarded and red brick on ground floor.

FURNACE MILL 2010

Two-storey plus attic with half-hipped plain tile gambrel roof. Two doubled cart doors to centre and left, plus central boarded loft door on first floor. Lean-to outshot to right. Attached to the right is a single-storey stable block with three strap-hinged half-doors and a one point eight metre high red brick wall that extends thirty metres with a gateway and linking to a red brick plain-tiled outhouse to the north of the mill.
Projecting from low in the left return side still remains the mill wheel axle, now in a dry pit.
The original internal flooring and some of the mill machinery still survive.

WATER WHEEL PIT AND AXLE 2010

The earliest reference to a grist mill on this site is 1285. Robert de Crowherst and Simon de Breglonde held half each. Simon lived at Badgers Row in Lamberhurst and was the village blacksmith (22).

A miller is named in the early Robertsbridge Abbey rentals for Hoathly (1280-1300) as one John de Molendio (22).

Alexander Collyn, in his will of 1552, left 'the Manor of Hoathly – a corn mill, an iron mill and a hammer mill'.

William Courtney Morland, the then Lord of the Manor of Lamberhurst, records in 1857 of writing to Arnold and Smith, who then owned the mill, 'for a price for grinding hog corn' (16).

The site is of great historical and archaeological importance as it was close by that the Lamberhurst Furnace, the largest working furnace and mill in the UK at one time, was situated.

PEPPERMILL (LONG WALK 1)

This was situated off Furnace Lane and east of Lamberhurst Furnace. First mentioned in the 1200s (4) as Pepperlonde.

Again recorded in 1568, which states that, 'a Mr Payne held one wood called Pepper Mill, wherein is a pond and sometime a mill [5] on land owned by Bayham Abbey.

**PEPPERMILL SLUICE & WATER WHEEL
IN DISREPAIR 1880s (78)**

The name may evolve from a Simon de la Puer de Pepperlonde, who is recorded as holding land west of Lamberhurst on the north bank of the River Teise (but no mention of a mill). Alternatively, it could derive from the fact that a rent paid in ground pepper was favoured by Robertsbridge Abbey (the then landlords), hence the term 'pepper rent'.
It was still in operation in the 18th century, as it is featured on a map of Lamberhurst of 1770.

BREWING – CIDER, BEER AND WINE (*circa* 1100-2009)

Cider Manufacture

Lamberhurst cider through the ages was recognised as high quality, with a distinctive strong spiced taste. The late Saxons, around 994-1013, would have erected huts or houses and planted the first apple trees, manufactured cider and formed the congregation of the first wooden church at Lamberhurst, in 998.

However, it was the Normans who brought profound changes to apple growing in Kent. They had a strong tradition of apple growing and cider making and introduced many new types of apple, especially the Pearmain, which was particularly valued for cider making.

A charter of 1137 indicates that the area that used to be known as 'Gerelody' (the triangular section of land between Town Hill, The Broadway and the River Teise, which is now occupied by Coggers Cottages and the shops) was utilised as an orchard to serve the village cider industry (3).

In 1138, Helyas de Crevecoeur, Lord of the Manor, in his grant to Leeds Priory, cites his 'mills, ovens and orchards in Lamberhurst' (3). The mills not only ground corn, but produced malt for beer and made cider from the orchards that then lined both banks of the River Teise. Another orchard was situated at Baker's den at the bottom of School Lane.

In 1240, a letter from the Prior of Combwell to the Abbot of Robertsbridge asks the Abbot for witnesses to a new lease for the baking and brewing workshop to the rear of Stair House. The de Scotneys ran this venture for the Prior until the 1250s.

In the early 1300s, William Palmer was manufacturing cider at 'Palmers Croft' (Murlingden), using water from a spring on the site that was said to give it its distinctive taste (1).

A will of 1487 states that a Nicholas Fowle had inherited 'one tenement in Lamberhurst, called Relfes' (Mill House). It had stopped trading by the early 1400s, but the water mill behind it continued to produce malt and cider.

APPLE ORCHARD   APPLE JUICE FROM THE PRESS

Two generations later, a will of 1519 states that a John Fowle had left the mill and the water wheel to his son Richard, who 'shall suffer my two [other] sons, John and Christopher, to grind their fruits to make cider so that it be their fruit and no other man's'.

In his will of 1525, Thomas Fowle left 'orchards and appulls for making cider'.

In the 1600s, the Fowle family took over Coggers Hall and revived the flagging cider industry, converting the

Fulling Mill to a cider press.

By the 1700s, the Thomas family of Coggers Hall had the monopoly of the manufacture and retail sale of cider and ale in the village (1).

Marjorie Edwards can still remember cider being produced at Whisketts Farm; the farmer was called Guest.

Beer Brewing

Many of the public houses brewed their own beer, but there is evidence of premises devoted to brewing beer and then selling on to the village pubs.

The Mulses was a brew house situated behind Rose Villas on the High Street, next to the River Teise, that serviced beer to the local pubs from the 1300s to the early 1800s, which at the latter date was the largest in Lamberhurst. Its name may have derived from the fact that it produced a poor man's mead, called 'Mulsa', an alcoholic sweetened water, a Lamberhurst speciality (1).

There is evidence that a brewery existed behind the Stair House as early as 1138, in a land grant to the church, where one Maurice the Brewer is recorded (66). Closed in the 1530s at the dissolution of the abbeys.

Smiths Brewery was established *circa* 1800 upon the closure of Ricarde's Toft, by Edward Smith of Wadhurst; it was the main brewery of the village in the 19th and 20th centuries and was situated on the current site of Morland Drive, behind Stair House (31).

The main brewery was located at the rear of Stair House, with storage of the beer barrels in the former upper and lower barns of Stair House (at the time, the massive medieval stone foundations were still in evidence).

F. Alan Simpson of Brenchley entered the business in 1839 and it was renamed Smith & Simpson. It included four tied public houses, three of which were The Fountain Inn, Tunbridge Wells; The White Hart, Rusthall; and The Station Inn, Tonbridge.

In 1847, it was recorded as being named Smith, Frederick and Thomas Brewers.

SMITHS BREWERY 1880 (78)

It became Smith & Co Lamberhurst Ltd in 1889, with directors recorded as Fred Smith, Thomas Smith and Philip Simpson, and employing ten men. Fred was living at Stair House, unmarried, with his widowed mother, brothers and sisters.

The brewery was extensively modernised in 1892, with new buildings and new, up to date brewing machinery. A coloured metal sign gives an excellent illustration of what it would have looked like at the time.

SMITHS BREWERY PICTURE *CIRCA* 1890s (78)

All four tied public houses were also modernised in the same year.
In 1908, it purchased the Hastings brewery, J. C. Burfield & Co and all their tied public houses.
By now, the driving force of the business was (Clement) Philip Simpson; his brother Alan was the Managing Director.
The successful entrepreneurs built up the business until they controlled fifty-four tied public houses, had constructed their own brick-built houses in Brewer Street to house their workers in the 1890s and installed their own generator that serviced the office, works, houses and some form of limited street lighting either side of the village bridge.

SMITHS BREWERY 1920 (78)

The actual brewery is to the rear left of the buildings; at the front centre and right was where the barrels were stored – see illustration on sign above)
One can imagine the shock in 1921 when Philip announced his early retirement. The reason for this was the introduction of the Weights and Measures Act of 1920, which would have meant the reduction in the strength of beer brewed by Smith & Co, which Philip would not do (68). Alan did not want to continue on his own, so in the same year fifty-four tied houses were sold for £134,610 and in the following year the brewery was sold to Dartford Brewery Co Ltd for an undisclosed sum.
In 1924, Style and Winch of Medway bought Dartford Brewery.
The last recorded brewing on the site was in 1935.

Wine Production

Small-scale wine production in Lamberhurst was recorded in 1909, when the trade of the shepherds 'vied with vine keeping' (52).
In 1971, Kenneth McAlpine and his farm manager Bob Reeves considered that some of the land they had just purchased on the west side of The Down, north facing but well sheltered from the prevailing south-westerly winds, would be an ideal location for a vineyard.
In 1972, 3.64 hectares were planted with Muller Thurgau, Seyval Blanc, and Madeleine Angevine. The vinery was built in 1974 and produced around 700 bottles of wine. Although the north-facing vines produced their crop two weeks later than south-facing vines, it was a distinct advantage in the early part of the growing season, as being later growing, it reduced the risk of potential frost damage (81).

LAMBERHURST VINEYARDS 2010

The vineyard was sold in 1994 and is now owned by English Wines plc, who also owns the Tenterden vineyard.
Currently it consists of 200 acres of Bacchus, pinot noir, rondo, regent and Ortega. However, wine is no longer made at Lamberhurst; the grapes are sent to Tenterden.
So continues the tradition of growing crops in Lamberhurst for the brewing industry, but following the new changes of taste.

CLOTH MANUFACTURING (*circa 1275-1620*)

Spinning and weaving had taken place in Lamberhurst on a small domestic scale in antiquity, as in most towns and villages, but never progressed beyond this to the finishing processes in the production of cloth, fulling and finishing (or 'dressing').

Then, around 1275, a yeoman named Robert Cogger moved to Lamberhurst. He was to build Coggers Hall in the village as his main seat, *circa* 1280, but, more importantly, single-handedly rescued the village from virtual economic collapse through the crash in the wool market. He realised that there was now a ready market for home-made woollen cloth and, instead of trying to export wool, he established the first cloth-making industry in the parish. He was one of the new breed entering the cloth industry at this time, leasing land which he farmed and sub-leased to other farmers, living off his farming returns and rents, with spare capital for investment in other ventures. He leased a large area of the Manor of Mayfield, south of the Lamberhurst to Wadhurst Road, from Whisketts Farm to Lady Mead, which was owned by the Archbishop of Canterbury's Manor of South Malling, near Lewes (6). Robert held this land through the mesne tenure of the de Scotney family.

He could be described as the first capitalist entrepreneur of Lamberhurst. He specialised in the production of 'Kentish broadcloth', which was the most valuable of the two types of cloth produced on the Weald, being a heavy, luxury cloth, produced in great quantities. The other was 'kersey cloth', which was inferior in quality and thickness. 'Broadcloth's' main markets were London and Western Europe.

There were statutory standards regarding its manufacture, which were a minimum length of 28 yards and minimum weight of 86 pounds, and was usually one and three quarter yards wide (48).

He styled himself as a 'clothier', who required numerous skills – the knowledge of wools, the art of dyeing and overall knowledge of the whole process of cloth manufacture, but his key skills were in management and entrepreneurship.

Whereas the prior processes were carried out domestically by women in farmhouses and cottages, or small establishments with little capital investment, fulling, particularly 'broadcloth', required capital investment to build the mills to provide the water power and machinery to carry out the process. Robert Cogger had this wealth.

13TH CENTURY FULLING MILL
With acknowledgement to Anne Marie Edwards

He built a water-powered Fulling Mill to the north-west of Coggers Hall, powered by the Gill Stream via a Mill Pond (1).

He would have purchased the raw wool locally and have had a very organised system of independent out-workers for the spinning and weaving processes, operating out of their houses in the village, and then carried out the fulling process in his own mill.

Fulling involved three processes: scouring, milling (thickening) and then stretching.

The first stage was to scour the cloth to rid it of its natural oils and greases that would have inhibited the binding actions of the dyes. This process involved smearing the cloth with Fullers earth (hence the process's name), which was mined at Maidstone, and immersing it in a trough of hot water and then labourers would trample the cloth underfoot.

The second milling stage was to consolidate the fibres of the cloth and produce a uniform thickness.

This process was to pass the cloth under water-powered hammers usually three times to remove all final remains of the natural wool grease and dirt, to strengthen and smooth the cloth and to thicken it by compressing and binding its fibres. The first time the trough would have contained urine, the second fuller's earth and the third hot soapy water, before a final thorough rinsing in clean water. Each pounding lasted two hours (58).

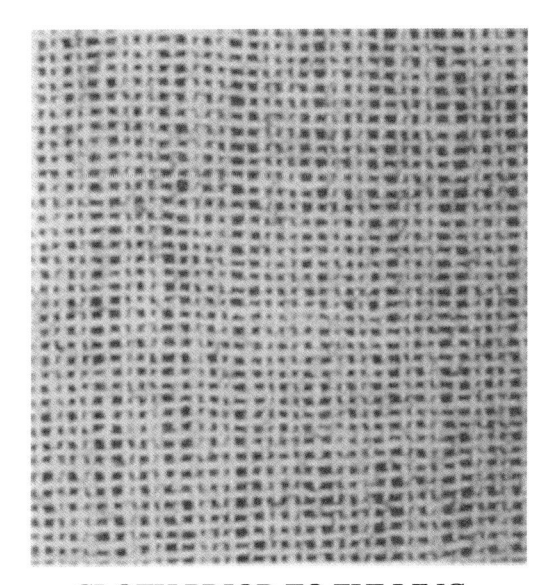

CLOTH PRIOR TO FULLING
Showing the open yarn of the fabric (56)

CLOTH AFTER FULLING
The yarns are more compact and even (56)

The stocks would have consisted of a wooden frame to support an inclined wooden shank and heavy wooden foot on the end, which was lifted by means of a tripped cam-shaft and allowed it to swing downwards in an arc onto the cloth in the trough. Usually, the stocks were set in pairs, working alternately. As can be seen in the illustration overleaf, the face of the foot had a stepped edge and this, along with the concave base of the trough, advanced the cloth after each blow, reducing the risk of over-pounding of sections (57).

FULLING STOCK ASSEMBLY (56)

Fulling was a skilled process and the fuller would have to take into account the type of wool, the type of water, the cloth texture, the temperature of the water and the time allowed under the fulling hammers. Any error would result in holes and the ruin of the whole bolt of cloth. The fulling process resulted in the cloth losing 10-20% of its size. Therefore, the final stage of manufacture in Lamberhurst, prior to dyeing, was subjecting the cloth to a process known as 'Tentering'.

The wet cloth was stretched on two parallel wooden upright frames similar to an open fence, built outside the mill, but near to it. The cloth was pulled evenly and hooked onto blunt-headed, upward-facing hooks driven at intervals into the top rail of the top frame and then onto the nails of the bottom adjustable frame, stretching it to the required size by adjusting it to the right tension, and then left to dry.

It also ensured even drying and bleaching of the cloth in the sunlight (23, 56, 57, 58).

'Taint Mead', behind Coggers Hall on the west bank of the Gill Stream, was where Robert Cogger organised the stretching of his unfinished wet cloth on 'tenters', or hooks (1). The term 'on tenterhooks' was so generated.

Then he would have put it out to individual dyers in the village and collected it back for the final 'finishing' or 'dressing' process, which raised the nap, by brushing it with teasel plant heads (similar to Scottish thistle seed heads) mounted on a wooden handle, and then the cloth was cropped to a uniform thickness with hand shears, which improved its appearance and feel by making it smoother (23, 56, 57, 58).

This would not have been carried out locally. His major market was selling untreated cloth to finishers in London or on the Continent (the latter under strict licence).

Transportation to his end-market would have been by pack horse to Tonbridge or Maidstone and then by boat to London via the River Medway and the River Thames to London or to the Continent via the Kent ports.

The wealth he accrued is confirmed by the will of his wife, in which she is listed as being liable to a one-off annual tax payment of four shillings, the highest that had ever been recorded by a Lamberhurst parishioner, other than gentry.

The cloth industry developed to be, along with iron manufacture, the most important industry in Lamberhurst.

It was still recorded as being in operation in 1501, in a Seminal Indenture, over two hundred years after its establishment, a 'fulling mill and mill pond on the Gill stream that flows through the garden [of Coggers Hall] to the rear'.

The Act of Parliament of 1566, which banned the export of unfinished cloth, must have been a catastrophic blow to the business.

A mill pond is recorded in 1568 on the Gill Stream behind Ricards, but no mill (5).

The lack of an entrepreneur of the stature of Robert Cogger in the late 16th and early 17th centuries caused the ultimate demise of the business. The almost continuous wars in Northern Europe, which was its predominant market, were drastic, but it was the demands of fashion for a lighter cloth that was its death knell. It appears that, instead of entering the emerging market for lighter, cheaper cloths, the Lamberhurst industry 'buried its head in the sand', stuck to what it knew and saw its business collapse (49).

The weaving industry in the village had followed the pattern in the rest of Kent, with the commercialism and expansion of the existing domestic industry. In the 1570s, commercial manufacture was established at the Tan House and Tiled Cottage on School Hill.

The Fulling Mill was converted to a cider press *circa* 1620. It is not illustrated on a map of the village of 1770, so it must have been demolished by then. No trace of it survives today; its foundations are under the new houses and rear gardens of Ricards Mews on the west side of School Hill.

ANIMAL HUSBANDRY: (*circa* 1280-1900)

As detailed in the previous chapter, the colonisation work of the Count of Eu, Robert de Crevecoeur and the Archbishop of Canterbury, Lords of the Manor, which resulted in the major forest clearings in and around Lamberhurst, plus the collapse of the market for wool in the 1280s and a new virulent disease of sheep, propelled the raising of cattle for beef into the stratosphere.

The horned 'red cows' that inhabited these forests in history, with their distinctive long strong horns, developed to the feeding requirements of its domain, were the catalyst for the development of the beef industry of Lamberhurst.

They were used as draft animals in their early years, before being primed for beef production at the age of six or seven.

They were bred for their speed in moving across difficult terrain, their hardiness when grazing on poor lands and their muscling, all ideally suited to the High Weald.

Over time, benefiting from substantially better pastures and selective breeding, they developed into the Sussex breed of cow, noted for their fineness of hide and for the closeness and delicacy of their meat, that became the major cattle breed of the Weald.

They were not merely valuable for their meat and hides. In the 1300s and early 1700s, the Manor of Lamberhurst sold a considerable amount of manure that was surplus to the village requirements. An average year's sales would have been enough then to have rented a one hundred acre farm.

SUSSEX BREED CATTLE (53)

It maintained its dominance for hundreds of years until the 1800s, when cross-breeding in Tees Water and Durham produced the Shorthorn. W. C. Morland recorded in his diaries of experimenting with different breeds of cattle, but Sussex and Shorthorns were his main stock (16).

Farms were still the main employers in the village in the 1880s; as the Census of 1881 records, over fifty farm labourer families were living here, working on 3525 acres in Kent and 1900 acres in Sussex (62).

WEEKLY MARKET, ANNUAL FAIR AND SLAUGHTER-HOUSES (1314-1720; 1314-1953; 1314-1464 and 1953-2001)

In 1198, Emma de Crevecoeur had a request to hold a market in Lamberhurst turned down by the then King, Richard I.

Over one hundred years later, on 1st June 1314, the request at last received royal approval, when Edward II's primate granted Walter Reynolds, the Archbishop of Canterbury (the king's firm favourite), the right to hold a weekly market on a Wednesday (on what is now The Broadway) and an annual fair on 21st May (on Fair Field, the land behind Chequers Oast) in Lamberhurst, as cattle was by now the village's most important staple product. The market started slowly, but by 1400 was regarded as paramount within this area of the High Weald (45) (49).

This area of the village was then called 'The Shambles', which derives from the Saxon word ''Fleshammels', meaning street of butchers, or the medieval word 'Shamel', meaning booths or benches on which meat was displayed (41). Booths, benches and cattle pens would have been set up on both sides of the road, displaying wares to be sold, in the area of the current Coggers Cottages.

This grant had massive repercussions on the development and population of Lamberhurst, which was recorded as having only one hundred inhabitants in 1280.

The Welsh drovers made Lamberhurst one of their overnight stopovers, lodging at Badgers Row, two cottages on the site that is now the War Memorial Hall, on their way to the summer pasturing for their cattle on Romney Marsh (1).

Also, as detailed earlier, cattle reared for their meat had replaced the raising of sheep for wool as the main agrarian activity and nowhere was available to slaughter them locally.

Consequently, a slaughter-house was established occupying the present site of Coggers Cottages, in the centre of the village, an area that was originally part of the market on 'Broadway'. In the 1430s, it is recorded that over one hundred cattle per week were slaughtered here (4).

Around 1475, a five-bay Wealden Hall House was built on the site of 'The Shambles', which was the Estate Manager's house of the Coggers Estate, and the abattoir closed. A small abattoir was opened at the lower end of Brewer Street in the 1950s, which was purchased by John Marshall, the butcher on Town Hill, in the 1970s. Marshall's Abattoir expanded to become one of the largest in the South of England, employing over one hundred people, slaughtering 4000 sheep per day and exporting to most countries in Western Europe. It closed in 2001, due to the effects of the foot and mouth epidemic (75). The site is now occupied by Hop Garden Close.

ANNUAL FAIR, EARLY 1950s (78)

The weekly market died out in the 1700s, but the fair continued, majoring on a cattle, sheep and horse auction as an annual feature, reputedly a colourful event.

Older residents can remember the chaos, prior to the introduction of cattle lorries, of bullocks and sheep being 'driven' on the roads by herdsmen, from miles around. Gypsies would come to sell their clothes pegs and their horses, which would be paraded and often galloped up and down the street.

Even with the introduction of transportation, chaos continued, with rows of cattle lorries lining The Broadway, which was still then the main road to Hastings, the A21, hindering the through traffic, especially when herds of bullocks or flocks of sheep escaped onto the road, when they were being loaded up (75).

ANNUAL FAIR, EARLY 1950s (78)

ANNUAL FAIR, EARLY 1950s (78)

The last annual fair was held on 5th April 1953.

LEATHER MANUFACTURE (1250-1550)

The establishment of The Shambles instigated the development of the vertical integration of the leather industry in the village.

Tanning vats were already situated at Murlingden and owned by the Wellere family, top stratum yeomen of Lamberhurst.

Also, a substantial stone workshop to dye the leather was already in use on the site currently occupied by Tanyard Cottages in the centre of the village and managed by Ralph the Dyer.

A curing workshop was built on the site now occupied by Tan House on Town Hill (the overseer, Stephen Tanner, lived at Riverside, minimum second generation of tanners).

Finished leather workshops were built next to the river behind the current Rose Villas site (called 'Molts') and on the site of the house that was formerly the Horse and Groom public house on Old Town Hill (1).

LEATHER SCRAPING THE HIDE (23)

Now within the confines of the village, the cattle were slaughtered, the hides tanned, then cured, then dyed and the leather used to manufacture boots, shoes, saddles and harnesses.

By the 1430s, they were all in the ownership of a Ralph Wellere and run by the Palmer family.

London merchants were purchasing large quantities of leather hides and finished leather goods from the Wellere family at this time.

By the early 1500s, a Stephen Palmer ran the tanning vats, but sold them to Robert and Thomas Ovynden (father and son) in the 1550s, when the former moved to London to become 'citizens and grocers'. Palmer's largest customer had been the White Canons of Bayham Abbey, so it would be of no surprise to learn that both were involved in the 'riot' of 1525 that temporarily reinstated the canons after Cardinal Wolsey had closed down Bayham Abbey (1).

The blood and tannin running down the streets of Lamberhurst and draining into the River Teise must have been substantial, hazardous and unhealthy.

Probably for this reason, by the 1550s, most of the leather trade was transferred to a large tannery outside the village, at Hook Green.

IRON MANUFACTURE AND FORGING (*circa* 1546-1782)

BACKGROUND AND INTRODUCTION

Although the Romans were extensive in iron ore mining and smelting, they tended to concentrate on the Lower Weald, with only sporadic venturing into the High Weald. There is evidence of them at Wadhurst, but there is no evidence, as yet, to suggest that they operated in Lamberhurst. I suspect that the then impenetrability of the High Weald precluded them.

The Jutes, Saxons and Normans also do not appear to have mined here.

However, the High Weald was in fact rich in iron ore deposits. The sandstone ridges of the area contain iron nodes with high phosphorus content, close to the surface; in fact, traces can still be seen today in the quarry face at Scotney Castle. It was not until the late 15th century, however, that this was exploited.

From this period up to the late 1700s, the High Weald, as quoted by John Moon, 'was the Black Country of the period. Smoke and flames from the various furnaces filled the sky and
dwellings within the vicinity felt the repeated shock waves of the forge trip hammers'.

A considerable number of excellent books have been written on the Wealden Iron Industry, so I do not intend to write generalistically on the subject, but to concentrate on the single site, local to Lamberhurst.

LAMBERHURST FURNACE AND FORGE

This site was at Hoathly, west of The Down, and named Lamberhurst Furnace. It had the benefit of local availability of iron ore, coppice wood cultivation for charcoal, water power supplied by the River Teise, local clay to line the furnace and make the moulds, chalk which acted as a flux, and marl, an alternative material for making the moulds.

Although the site was ideal, it was recorded as a topographical miniature of Lamberhurst and raises the question of why it was not sited in Lamberhurst village? I suspect the answer is down to two main reasons. Firstly, Lamberhurst then was a thriving industrial village, with a slaughter-house, tanning operations, leather working and beer and cider brewing; adequate, available space would have been limited. Secondly, why would its inhabitants want to add to the stench and filth of the leather industry, the pollution, noise and disruption of an ironworks? The siting at Hoathly was close enough to Lamberhurst to have a positive effect on its prosperity, but away from the village nucleus so that it did not suffer from its adverse effects.

ARTIST'S RECONSTRUCTION OF A BLAST FURNACE (26)
With acknowledgement to West Sussex County Council, Mike Codd and PPL Limited

The cut-away view shows the water wheel powering two sets of bellows to provide a continuous blast of air to the furnace hearth and to a device to bore out cast cannon. The molten iron is being run into a pit, which would have held a vertical mould for casting cannon.

It was established to predominantly produce cannon, as opposed to wrought iron bar for blacksmiths to produce tools, nails, etc, which was the main role of most other Wealden furnaces at the time.

Henry VIII had made war on France in 1542 and armaments were in great demand, from limited sources. This was the first of five wars over the next one hundred and thirty years that were to prove to be 'bouquets and brickbats' for the Lamberhurst Furnace. During the war years, demand was excessive and profits huge, but during the non-war years demand was non-existent and would have spelled the death of the furnace, had it not converted manufacture to produce iron skillets, fire backs, oven doors and wrought iron bar; the famous 'boom and bust cycle'.

ARTIST'S RECONSTRUCTION OF AN IRON FOUNDRY (26)
With acknowledgement to West Sussex County Council, Mike Codd and PPL Limited

The cut-away view of a Wealden Forge shows the forge or finery reheating iron bar and the trip hammer shaping the bar, both powered by separate water wheels.

The furnace was used for all three stages in the production of cannon. The first 'heat' reduced the iron ore at a much higher temperature than the traditional bloomery process, to liquid iron that flowed into a network of sand channels to cool. It was then subject to two further 'heats' to remove its carbon content and to produce a grade of iron that was of sufficiently high quality to produce cannon.

The mould for the cannon would have been sited vertically in a pit in front of the furnace (as illustrated on previous page) that would have been dug and then backfilled with tightly packed earth to keep the mould steady during the pour (25).

When producing iron for bar or other manufactured products, after its first 'heat', it would have then gone to the 'finery', which was a separate manufacturing station where the iron was re-melted to remove its carbon content and then hammered to expel any slag while still hot. It would then have gone to the 'chafery' for its final stage of manufacture. It was here that it was formed into bar, normally three metres in length, by means of a very heavy trip forge hammer head. The bar would have then been used to manufacture implements on site or sold in its raw bar state to local blacksmiths for reworking.

The power for the ironworks was water which was supplied via a newly cut leat from the River Teise (known as the Great Ditch) to the water wheels for the furnace, finery and chafery.

Delivery of cannon to Maidstone, for then transporting to London by boat, via the River Medway and River Thames, was only possible during the early summer. The River Teise, particularly due to its considerable number of weirs, was unsuitable, and the clay-based roads were almost impassable in winter to all traffic, but especially to two-ton cannon being transported by an ox-drawn wagon.

No detail survives of the original ironworks layout or operation, but does of the substantial rebuild of 1695. Two maps of 1770 and 1795 give interesting details.

SITE PLAN 1770

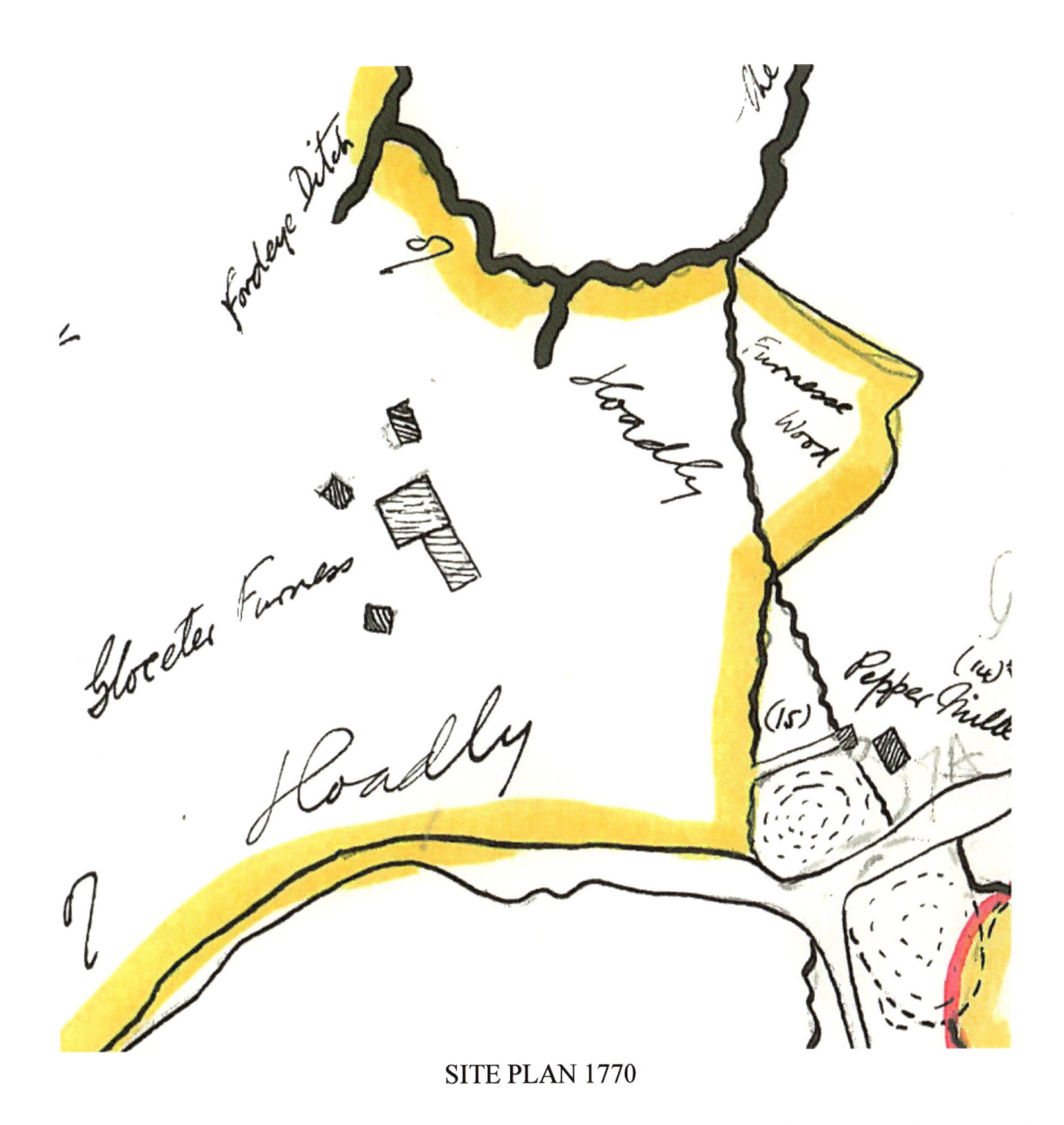

In the centre of the site was the furnace, finery and chafery, to the north was the counting house, to the north-west was the 'coaltackplace' (building for storing coal which had by now replaced charcoal as fuel) and to the south the 'boreing houfe' (where the casting was bored out to form a cannon).

There would also have been storage space for the ore and stables for the oxen used for hauling ore, coal, clay and finished cannons. The manager's house, garden and cherry orchard were to the north of the furnace site.

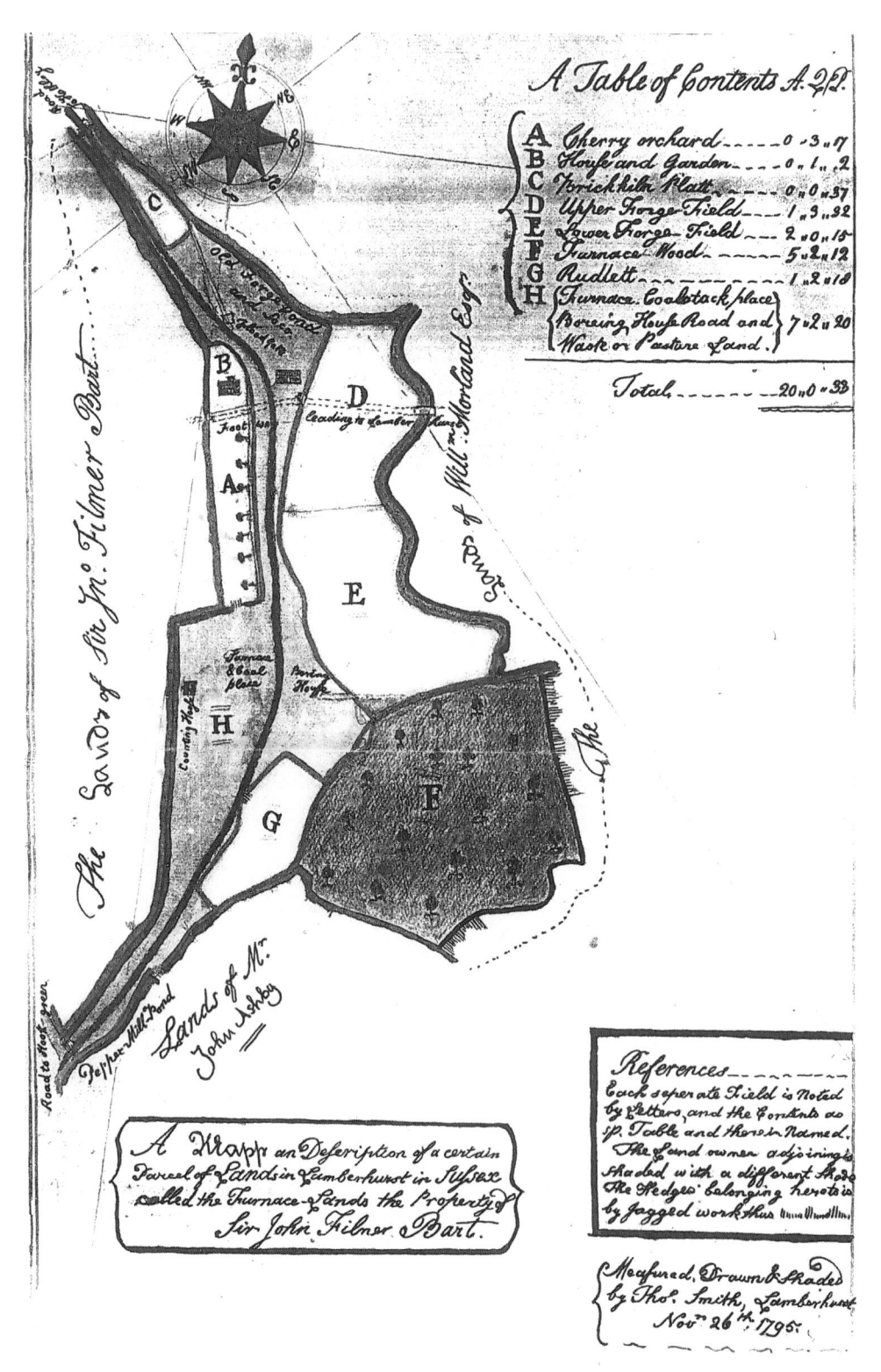

SITE PLAN 1795 (78)

It would therefore have been a centralised manufacturing centre in its own right.

The repercussions of its establishment on employment locally were great. The furnace would have needed woodcutters initially (for cutting the coppice wood, to make charcoal); carriers; ore, chalk and clay miners; as well as the skilled men on site, such as the founders, finers, chafers and borers.

The land on which the furnace was built was originally owned by the church. The Abbey of Robertsbridge leased the land for peppercorn rent of 'one red rose per day on St John the Baptist's Day' to the collegiate church of St Peter's of Lingfield in Surrey (7).

However, in 1546, The Manor of Hoathly was sold to Thomas Cawarden by Henry VIII, after wresting it from the church in the Reformation. Thomas was one of Henry's favourites, supporting him in his religious Reformation. He was a gentleman of the Privy Chamber, Master of the Revels and keeper of the king's tents. He fought with Henry in the capture of Boulogne and was knighted. He was Lord of the Manor of Hextalls, Bletchingley, near Croydon (27).

The minutes of the commission set up in 1547 by the Duke of Somerset, 'Protector of the Realm' and uncle of the boy king Edward VI, to investigate 'The question of the new iron works on the Weald and the effect of depleting timber stocks on other trades', gives a definitive dating to the establishment of the original ironworks.

This commission invited anyone, individuals or business owners, to voice their complaints and concerns and then to make a ruling on future action. One of the actual commissioners, Thomas Darell (who also held Scotney Castle), complained as follows: 'Alexandre Collyn had built a furnace at Lamberhurst and had bought timber rights from Sir John Gresham and has apparently felled all the oak trees and is now starting on the beeches. He has also diverted a stream [the River Teise] to power the water hammer at the furnace. And moreover for the conveyance of water for the maintaining of the same hammer the same Alexander Collyn hath caused a great ditch to be made by estimation in length of 3 or 4 furlongs to Hoathb[l]y'. The former stream bed had acted as a property line for landowners and was the county boundary between Kent and Sussex. The commission made no ruling and when the problem was again raised during the reign of Elizabeth I, restrictions were placed on the removal of trees throughout England, but the Weald was made exempt from this law.

Straker confirms the river cut in more detail: 'to serve the needs of the forges, a straighter course was cut, both at Lamberhurst Forge and [in] Brown's Wood. It cut a straight course across a bend in the River Teise, through a slight rise in the ground. The length is about 1300 yards and, as the stream in its course round the bend falls considerably, a good head of water was obtained without a high bay. There is only a slight widening of the cut, hardly to be called a pond.' There was therefore no hammer pond on the site.

So Collyn would have leased the land from Cawarden and built the first furnace prior to 1547 (24). (I think the later dating of its establishment; refer to substantial rebuilding work, especially in the cases where the furnace would have laid dormant during the lows in the market.) He must have been a forward thinking and rich individual. He would have foreseen the escalation in demand for cast cannon and had the resources to finance the building and fitting out of the new blast furnace.

Large-scale production would have started immediately, due to this explosion in the market requirements for cannon, attributed to three main factors (24):

1) A breakthrough in cannon manufacturing design by William Levett at Buxted in Marefield parish in 1543, with the casting of the first one-piece cast cannon (which was solid cast and then bored out).
2) The immigration of experienced French workers from the iron-working district of Pays de Bray. The earliest came to England about 1490, rising steadily until in the 1560s half the furnace and forge workers of the Weald had migrated from France to England.
3) England was at war with France: 1542-1546, 1549-1550; which required naval cannon and cannon for the new forts that Henry VIII commissioned for defending the Kent coast against possible invasion. This was supplied to the admiralty, but also much was illegally exported to Europe. Casting iron cannon was much more profitable than the making of 'sows' or lengths of iron for refining.

The change of sovereignty and religion in 1553 had a devastating effect on Sir Thomas Cowerden. He was systematically persecuted, and then finally prosecuted for his alleged involvement in the Peasants Revolt. He was stripped of all his lands and died in the Tower of London in 1559 (27).

In his will of 1552, Alexander Collyn left 'the Manor of Hoathly—a corn mill, an iron mill and a hammer mill' (plus 108 acres of land) freehold to his son, Stephen. Alexander must therefore have purchased the manor and the ironworks from the Crown.

Between 1548 and 1574, profits more than doubled and assisted the early retirement of Stephen Collyn from the business during the 1580s to become a landed gentleman. In 1582, he leased Coggers Hall from the Manor of Lamberhurst and made it his 'country seat', and then went on to lease vast areas of the village from Scotney Manor.

In 1584, during the reign of Elizabeth I, he sold the Manor of Hoathly to Sir Edward Filmer for £1,550. The family continued to hold the land well into the 19th century (37).

After 1588, the threat of the Armada had passed and Admiralty orders all but dried up. It therefore switched production to agricultural rollers and to domestic items such as oven doors and fire backs, which were becoming very popular due to the building of new dwellings with chimneys and fireplaces and the conversion of existing dwellings which only had smoke bays (24).

OVEN DOOR 2010

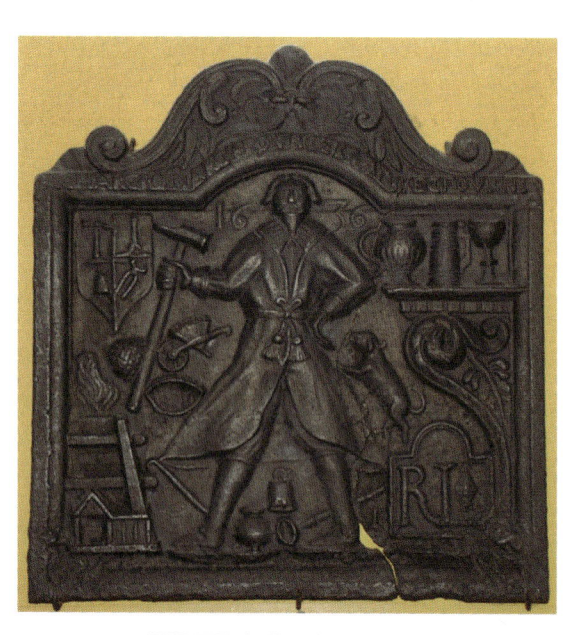

FIREBACK 2010

During the Civil War, 1642 to 1649, trade in armaments boomed again, particularly as Parliament secured the Wealden iron works, reflecting the political sympathy of the local area. The Dutch Wars of 1652-1667 and 1672-1674 boosted the income of the Saunders family during their tenure of Hoathly (24). After the end of this war, demand for armaments again slumped and production switched back to domestic items. Culinary items cast in iron called 'skillets' were manufactured at Hoathly by the Rummins family of Lamberhurst. The family name sometimes appears as a raised casting on the base of these utensils. During the 17th century it was leased to Thomas Saunders of Wadhurst (24).

'New men' with 'new money' were now entering the industry. These new affluent country gentry were typified by William Benge of Wadhurst, who purchased the iron works in 1695 for £470 and substantially rebuilt it. Benge and his family lived in a magnificent house, Faircrouch, in the town of Wadhurst (28).

Lamberhurst Furnace was re-named Gloucester Furnace in honour of the Duke of Gloucester, the son of the then Princess Anne (later to become Queen Anne), who both visited it in 1697, when lodging in Tunbridge Wells. From 1695, after refurbishment, it became the biggest furnace in England, producing more than 320 tons of iron per annum. Unfortunately, Benge was not in the same league as Alexander or Stephen Collyn; he misread the market and was declared bankrupt. He was buried in Wadhurst churchyard and his legacy is the cast-iron slab in the church floor, one of thirty still in evidence.

Lamberhurst Furnace's great claim to fame was that it produced the half mile of iron railings that surrounded Sir Christopher Wren's new St Paul's Cathedral of 1708, which were delivered and erected between 1710 and 1714. The furnace was then joint-owned by a Peter Gott, who had already made his fortune in iron foundering, and also had an involvement in all other working furnaces in the Weald, ten in Sussex and Hoathly, the largest of them all and the only one still working in Kent. His partner was Sir William Wellere, a Parliamentary general during the Civil War, whose family had moved to the area in 1324. It was let to Messrs Legas and Harrison.

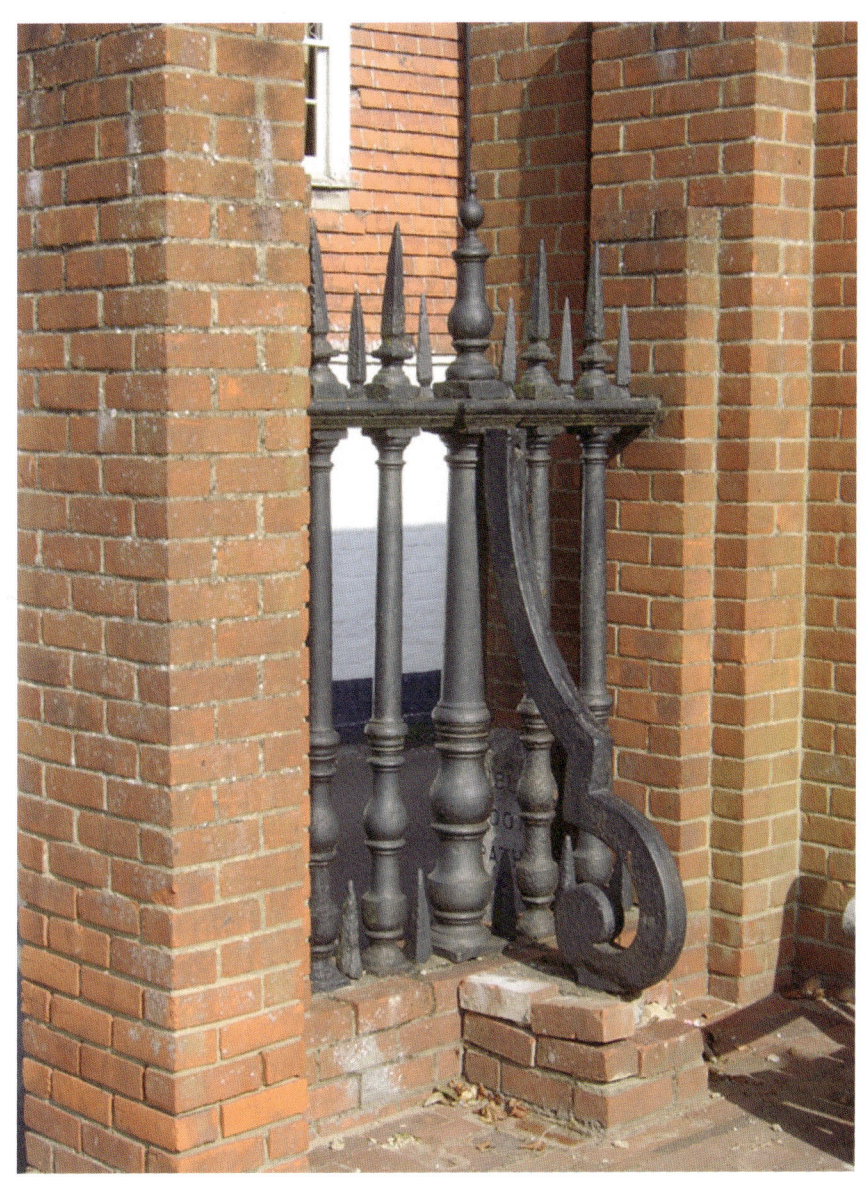

ST PAUL'S CATHEDRAL SHOWING THE
ORIGINAL IRON RAILINGS AND GATES (12)

The size of the contract was why it was carried out at Hoathly.
Hasted enthusiastically wrote in 1782, 'the iron rails around St Paul's churchyard were cast in this furnace. They compose the most magnificent balustrade perhaps in the universe, being the height of 5 feet 6 inches, in which there are at intervals 7 iron gates of beautiful workmanship, which together with the rails weigh 200 tons 81 lbs, the whole of which cost 6d per pound and with other charges amounted to the sum of £11,202 0s 6d.' This figure was taken from the books of the furnace and excluded transportation, design and erection charges, which are shown in the account records of St Paul's.
However, Sir Christopher Wren was not at all impressed, having preferred the lighter Italian or French style and designed them himself. He wrote, 'As to the iron fence it was wrested from me, and the doing of it carried out in such a way that I venture to say will ever be condemned'.
The fence was designed by a Richard Jones, who was the agent of Peter Gott, who had the full approval of the government and the Church Commission, in designing it, rather than Wren. There followed years of lies, recriminations, sackings and the hiding of facts. It is ironic that today little of the original fencing and gates produced at the Hoathly Furnace for the cathedral are *in situ*. Over the years it has been dismantled and distributed to various other sites, such as High Park, Toronto (63), Hastings and Lewes, or sold as scrap. A section is still in

place, mounted on a Portland stone base. There is also no reference to this original fencing on the current cathedral web site; it appears that everything about the unhappy saga has been systematically 'buried'.

The death of the furnace and forge was gradual and due to a number of factors. From the 1660s, its prices were undercut and its quality bettered by imports, especially from Sweden. The steeply rising price of fuel in competition with the local cloth and hop industries, due to a series of dry winters which decimated local coppice management that produced cord wood suitable for the manufacture of charcoal, was another factor. (In 1665, Tott Wood and East Wood, within the Manor of Lamberhurst alone, were described as 'not being well used'.) The substitution of pit coal for the expensive charcoal in 1735 also had a catastrophic effect. However, the loss of the valuable Admiralty contract to the Carron Ironworks in Scotland was the final blow (24).

The furnace was sketched by Swedenborg in 1724 and appeared in his book *De Ferro*, and contained the following description: 'This furnace was 28 feet high, 4 feet higher than any other in England. The greatest size inside was 7½ feet by 8 feet. For cannon, the hearth was made 5 feet long and 18 inches wide, for ordinary work 4 feet long and 18 inches wide.'

Its furnace was a permanent structure made of local sandstone and brick, square at the base and tapered towards its open top (24).

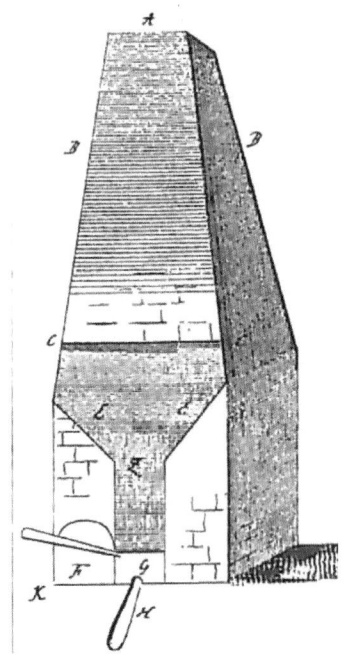

It is the only authentic illustration in existence.
In 1749, John Fuller noted that 'Hoathly was the only furnace out of the five remaining, apart from my own, which could make great guns'.
However, Legas had made a fortune, leaving £30,000 when he died in 1752.
A Mr Richard Tapsell, who married Legas's niece, sunk all his money into the furnace and then went bankrupt in 1765.

SWEDENBOURG SKETCH (24)

It was the end for the furnace. Straker confirmed this when he stated that, 'Lamberhurst [Furnace] finally closed in 1765. The forge seemed to have remained at work somewhat later than the furnace, probably working up scrap iron for local needs.'

In 1782, Hasted noted that, 'it was the only working foundry in Kent'; this probably refers to the forge only.

In 1787, it was recorded as 'yet standing and possibly may work again in case of war' (24).

The cast iron beam that supported the furnace structure above the casting arch was removed and built into the structure of Hoathly Farmhouse in 1795.

CAST IRON BEAM FROM THE LAMBERHURST FURNACE
With acknowledgement to Jeremy Hodgkinson, *The Wealden Iron Industry*

Much of the stone of the redundant furnace structure was re-used in 1800, on the front of the same house.
In 1976, one of the sections of the original railings of St Paul's Cathedral was re-sited on the front side of the Lamberhurst Memorial Hall, where it can still be seen today; it is Grade II Listed.
Two fire backs made at the Lamberhurst Furnace are now on display at Tunbridge Wells Museum.
East of Hoathly Mill on the right-hand side of the drive over the barbed-wire fence, is a depression in the ground. This dry ditch was the new 'leat' that was cut in the hillside to provide a head of water to the water wheel that powered Lamberhurst Furnace and Forge.
Nothing remains of the buildings, but if you walk a little further, you will come to a clearing on the right. This has been proposed as the actual site of the furnace (84).

HOP GROWING (1500-1950)

A considerable number of excellent books have been written on the Kent Hop Industry, so I do not intend to write generalistically on the subject, but to concentrate on the industry in Lamberhurst.

Hops first started being grown in Lamberhurst probably in the 16th century, when they first started being used in the brewing of beer (prior to this, ale was drunk which was made from malt and honey).

Historically, hop gardens were located on the entire Teise valley of Lamberhurst on its fertile sandstone soils and also on two of its ridges.

HOP PICKERS, FAIRFIELD, CHEQUERS FARM 1900 (78)

The fields on the north bank of the River Teise, opposite the rear of Coggers Cottage on the Broadway (last hop grower was Charlie Prickett of Coggers Farm in the 1950s), and Fair Field and the land behind The Chequers were the main areas.

COGGERS FARM OASTS ON BREWER STREET 1929 (78)

PICKED HOPS BEING TAKEN FOR DRYING, CHEQUERS FARM 1900 (78)

These hops would have been dried and sacked in the four Oast houses that were part of and situated behind and to the right of Coggers Farmhouse on the opposite bank of the river on Brewer Street. They were still there in 1955, recorded on a photograph taken by Thomas Frith.
They were demolished in the 1970s and replaced by houses.

INTERIOR OF ONE OF THE OAST HOUSES ON
BREWERY LANE, PART OF COGGERS FARM 1900s
(dried hops are on the floor) (78)

Whisketts Farm, opposite the entrance to Scotney Castle, south of the village, Down Farm, opposite the present Brown Trout public house, and Ridge Farm, on The Down, also grew hops.

Acreage given over to hops was 257 on the Sussex side of the village, in 1835 (61).

Kent-grown hops secured a higher price than Sussex-grown hops and an interesting story is recorded in the second half of the 1900s. The then farmer at Down Farm approached William C. Morland, the Lord of the Manor, to enquire if he could rent the half-acre area of Great Brooms Island (original site of the Norman East Mill). Although it was well set on the south Sussex bank, it had always been regarded as being in Kent. Morland agreed, the farmer planted a few hop bines on the site and then sold his entire crop as Kent hops, securing a better price (16).

The earliest remaining Oast house in Lamberhurst still exists on The Down, although little of the original structure survives.

It was the village's largest seasonal crop and required an enormous army of temporary workers.

Every September, the hops were ready to be picked and initially casual workers from Kent, particularly local Romany gypsies, would come with their whole families to pick them.

Hop picking would be the mid-term task of the Romanies; moving from farm to farm in summer, they would pick cherries, strawberries, blackcurrants, peas and beans, before moving to hops and then on to top fruits (apples and pears), before concluding with potatoes, prior to finding a place to stop for winter.

By the early 20th century, the East Enders of London replaced the Romanies as the main source of itinerant labour. Families would make their way to London Bridge Station and come down on 'hopper special' trains, which ran at unusual hours so as not to interrupt the main service. The hoppers would travel to Wadhurst and Goudhurst railway stations, then walk or get to Lamberhurst in wagons that farmers would send to collect them and their belongings. They treated the picking season as their holiday in the country, away from the grime, smoke and overpopulation of the capital (29).

They would stay in lodgings in the village or in blocks of specially built hoppers' huts. One set was situated on 'The Slip', an area now occupied by the new Pearse Place houses off Town Hill. A second set, plus a detached cook house, which are still there, are situated along the footpath leading from the end of the road on Brewer Street.

HOPPER HUTS 2010

Each 'hut' consisted of a double-room, single-storey unit, with brick walls and corrugated iron roofs. They were built in blocks so pickers could share communal washing and cooking facilities. The inside of the huts were usually adorned with personal belongings, to make their huts feel like home, and also contained 'faggot' beds, which were made from sticks. Entire families shared one unit for their six-week stay (30).
Marjorie Edwards, of Chester House, The Broadway, remembers them before the Second World War. 'They were a happy, but roughish bunch. They used to go to the Chequers and sing songs underneath their hurricane lamps, as they were very afraid of the dark. They used to take their Sunday roasts to Avards the bakers of the village [still there on the High Street]. Unfortunately, local shops had to put wire netting over their counter goods as they would regularly try to steal, but we used to look forward to them coming down and it was sad when they stopped.'

HOP GARDENS AT THE REAR OF THE CHEQUERS 1933 (78)
(The lower part of the photograph shows the hops harvested, the bines
taken away and the hop poles taken down)

The boom years for the Lamberhurst hop industry were the 1880s and 1890s.
From 1908, the brewers were importing more and more hops from Europe, particularly Germany.
After the Second World War, the East Enders stopped coming down, as machinery took over from hand picking and imports continued to rise, until they eclipsed the domestic production of hops. The glorious days of hop picking in Lamberhurst finally came to an end in the 1950s, the last being at Forstall Farm.
Scotney Castle Natural Trust, just outside the village, still grows hops to make their own brewed 'Scotney Ale'.

CLOCK AND WATCH MAKERS (1770-1830)

During the late 1700s and early 1800s, Lamberhurst was famous as an area for producing high quality watches and long-case clocks, by two principal individuals: Benjamin Reeves and Joseph Ballard.

Examples of their work today are rare and highly prized and command very high prices at auction.

Benjamin Reeves made watches and long-case clocks from the 1770s to 1790, at Campers on School Hill. He must have been good and successful in his business, as he is recorded as repairing the Battle church clock in 1774: some distance to travel during that period. He also owned numerous properties; as well as Campers in the village, he owned Tudor Cottage and Grantham Hall Farm and is recorded in 1775 as selling a leasehold house and lands in Heathfield and Burwash to a farmer, Thomas Morris, living in the former town (40). I speculate this was where he moved from to live in Lamberhurst. One of his descendants has a long-case clock manufactured by Benjamin that has been passed down over the generations.

Joseph Ballard was another watch and long-case clock maker who lived in the village from the late 1700s and the first half of the 1800s. Dolphin Cottage on the High Street was where he lived and Mansard House, next door, his workshop. He was more of a watch and clock assembler rather than a maker, as he bought in the actual movements and assembled them, but did paint the black Roman numerals on the white metal faces by hand, onto pencil tracings. The wooden outers for the case clocks were supplied by Thomas Rumens, who made them at Riverside House.

A pocket watch he manufactured in 1789 and a case clock dated 1830 are held in private collections (1).

WATCH (13)　　　　　　　　　　　　　　　　　　　CLOCK LONG CASE (13)

CONSTRUCTION

We already know that a stonemason had an established business on the lower High Street in the 1730s. Also, the construction business of Wallis, in the village, built the bridges and embankments when Spray Hill was established in the 1750s (69).

By the 19th century, construction had grown to be probably the largest industry and certainly the biggest employer in the village.

In the 1851 Census, a John Grigsby is recorded as a Mason and Bricklayer, employing five men.

In the 1881 Census, Edward Padgham is recorded as running a woodworking and joinery business, operating out of the Old Mill on High Street, who undertook all the restoration work in the church and the new-build school. The business must have been very prosperous, as the family owned half the village, including the Post Office (69).

By the time of the later Census, the industry had expanded rapidly, with ten bricklayers recorded as living here.

SADDLERS
Tile House on School Hill was a saddle and harness maker's shop.
First cited in a charter of 1544 (4).

TILE HOUSE 1880, with Arthur Winder in the doorway (78)

It was still in business in the 17th and 18th centuries and was recorded as a Saddler and Harness Maker in the 1881 Census, employing fifteen craftsmen; its largest customers were the Bayham and Scotney estates (16). This followed the trend of the time of estate workers leaving their jobs, establishing their own specialist businesses and trading with their former employers.
Its last known saddler was Arthur Winder.

HOP STRING MANUFACTURE
Twyman's factory was situated where the unoccupied single-storey shop is now, on the left-hand side of Victoria Stores at the bottom of the High Street.
Two cord winders are recorded as living in the village in 1881.
In the 1940s, with the decline of the local hop industry, the business was moved to Canterbury (32, 64).
It was demolished in 1956.

CHEMICAL MANUFACTURE

The Crown Chemical Company was established at Stair House on School Hill in 1948, with ten staff and directors. It moved here from London, as its small manufacturing unit had been destroyed by bombing in the Second World War.

It had been originally established there in the 1920s by a Hungarian who already operated the largest chemical factory in Europe at Ujpest.

Initially, only the offices and a laboratory were here, but the chemists developed new products and substantially improved existing products, which led to the subsequent development of manufacturing on the old site of Smiths Brewery.

When it closed in 1987, it was the largest manufacturer of veterinary pharmaceuticals in England and was the biggest employer in the village (31).

CROWN CHEMICAL CO 1987 (78)

OTHER RETAIL TRADES

PUBLIC HOUSES

History records nine public houses in Lamberhurst, which may initially seem an unusually large number for a village. However, up until the mid-20th century, this would have been common in most towns and villages, as, up to the building of the first turnpikes, travel would have been possible in summer, but impossible in autumn and winter, due to the effect of rain on the clay tracks, so villagers would have remained in their own village. Also, the favoured drink would initially have been cider, then ale, then beer, all of which were brewed in the village, at the mills, specialised breweries or at the back of the pubs.

(Please refer to the book *Lamberhurst: Jewel of the High Weald – A History* for details on specific Public Houses).

BUTCHERS

The trade must have been around in antiquity and certainly in existence after the establishment of a slaughter-house on The Broadway in 1314.

In 1840, two butchers are recorded: James Durrant and John Noakes (21).

In the late 1800s and early 1900s, two butchers are again recorded. Gurrs operated out of three different locations in the late 1800s and the first half of the 20th century.

William Gurr moved to the village from Chatham and continued his father's trade. All his shops were open-fronted and had meat hanging from hooks outside; what would the Health & Safety Executive think of that now!

GURRS BUTCHERS SHOP ON TOWN HILL *CIRCA* 1860 (70)

Originally he occupied a site that is now where Tuttysham flats are, on The High Street.
He then moved to Coggers Farmhouse on The Broadway, with his shop on the left-hand side of the building; in the 1871 Census he was described as 'a butcher, farmer, and hop grower'.
The business finally moved to what is now Walsingham's on Town Hill in 1902.

GURRS BUTCHERS SHOP ON THE BROADWAY CIRCA 1880 (70)

He not only owned Walsingham's, which had a slaughter-house behind and several sheds, one which produced sausages, but also four cottages above and considerable pasture land behind (70). The slaughter-house is still there; the cattle were slaughtered on the ground floor and were lifted up by chains and a pulley to the roof (a later ceiling has been added, but the original chains are still there).

William Gurr died in 1903 and the business was run by his widow and her eldest son Ernie, who was seventeen years old. She reportedly ruled with a rod of iron (70).

Ernie Gurr took over the business fully after his mother's death in 1930. He is always remembered for his trotting horse teams, which won him prizes at the Tunbridge Wells and Edenbridge shows (64). He remained a bachelor all his life.

Peter Sands, who worked here in his early career, can remember that deliveries to customers were by a high-stepping pony, called Mr Chips, and a lightweight trap. He would also give the village children free rides to Bayham Abbey.

ERNIE GURR AND MR CHIPS (70)

John Marshall then took over the business; the abattoir was still at the back, the butchers shop in the house and the huge inglenook fireplace was used as the 'check out'.
He also established another slaughter-house on Brewery Street.
He became ill in the 1970s and closed the butchers business.
Atkins was another butcher, originally situated on Town Hill at Hill House, next to Gurrs.
There is still a butchers shop in Lamberhurst today. Peter Sands is the heart and the information centre of the whole village, sited on The Broadway, that was originally a Wealden Hall House and was, for some time, 'The Red Lion'.
Peter was a butcher boy for Atkins, then apprentice butcher for Ernie Gurr for five years, graduating and becoming a master butcher himself. Then, when Atkins became ill in the 1970s, he purchased the business and transferred it to its present site.
In 2010, Peter sold the business, but continues to manage the shop, extending his 51 years as a butcher in the village.

PETER SANDS 2010

GENERAL STORES

Victoria House Stores

The first general store in the village was established by George and Charlie Reeve here in 1870.

The ground floor of the former house was converted to a greengrocers and a gentleman's and ladies' outfitters and next door (currently Peter Sands butchers) a haberdashery; the current plate glass windows were fitted in the 1900s. A single-storey addition to the left, which was the hardware department (now empty), was later added. It did not sell shoes.

It sent around a salesman to each house in the village to take an order for goods that were delivered later in the week by delivery boys on bicycles with a delivery basket on the front.

The gentry were treated differently: they would arrive in all their splendour in a chauffeur-driven horse and carriage and used to sit on a chair, giving the order to the staff, who loaded it into the carriage, while the chauffeur attended to the horses.

The current Post Office was the site of the gentleman's clothing department managed by George and it also had a ladies' clothing department. It employed six staff plus the brothers.

It stayed in the hands of the Reeve family for over one hundred years until the 1970s (64).

VICTORIA STORES 1887 (78)

Today it is one of the most successful traditional village stores in the area, comprising of a Post Office, newsagent, stationers, dry cleaners, greengrocers, confectioners, as well as selling meats, frozen fish, frozen and canned vegetables, jams, bread, pet food, snacks and coffee, and also providing a photocopying service.

VICTORIA STORES 2010

Manorden
In 1902, when he moved his butchers shop to Town Hill, William Gurr purchased the building and established a business that occupied the centre and right-hand side of the ground floor and named it Lamberhurst Stores.

GURRS GENERAL STORES 1902 (70)

It offered a tailoring service, sold ladies' and gentlemen's clothing and hats, groceries, tea, soaps, biscuits and confectioneries.
Probably closed on the death of William or latest 1930 upon the death of his wife.

Upway House
William Evans moved his family here from Wales in 1920 and purchased the property outright from the last Lord of the Manor of Lamberhurst, Colonel Henry Morland.
He established a business named Evans Lamberhurst Stores, which was a bustling, lively, very busy shop. In those days there were no self-service supermarket shelves or bar codes; customers were served individually and purchases rung into a till, goods were stacked on shelves behind the counter and it was the days of cocoa, Horlicks, home-made jams and specialist powders; there was no frozen food or pre-packed goods. Flour, biscuits and tea were purchased in bulk and broken down to individual customer requirements. In the back of the building was a shoe shop selling ladies' and gentleman's shoes, but did not sell clothing.
It operated a delivery service like Victoria House Stores, and employed two girls in addition to William and William Junior (63).

EVANS GENERAL STORES, OUTSIDE 1950s (78)

When William retired, the business was taken over by his son, William Junior, and remained in business until the 1970s, when he retired and the business was closed after fifty years of trading.

EVANS GENERAL STORE, INSIDE 1950s (78)

VARIOUS

By the 1840s, Lamberhurst had developed into a multi-industry and retail village.
Pigot records the following:
3 Blacksmiths, 2 Boot and Shoe Makers, 3 Carpenters, 1 Cooper, 1 Corn Factor, 6 Grocers, Drapers and General Stores, 2 Millers, 4 Hat Makers (none recorded in Brenchley, Goudhurst, Matfield or Horsmonden), 2 Saddlers, 3 Taylors, 1 Wheelwright, 1 Watchmaker, 1 Brick Maker, 1 Horse Dealer, 1 Brewer and 1 Glove Maker.
In total, including the above, in the 1840s there were twenty industries or manufacturers operating in Lamberhurst.
By the time of the 1861 Census, this had grown even further to thirty-six industries. Farming was still the biggest employer, with thirty-six farm labourers recorded, and shoe and bootmakers the biggest number of listings at ten.

HISTORICAL CHARTS

LORDS OF THE MANOR OF LAMBERHURST

YEARS	725-740	740-747	747-1066	1066-1090	1090-1266	1266-1540	1540-1542	1542-1606	-1608-1733	-1733-1934
LORDS OF THE MANOR										
AETHELBERHT II KING OF KENT	■									
AETHELBALD KING OF MERCIA		■								
BISHOPS OF ROCHESTER			■							
BISHOP ODO OF BAYEUX				■						
THE DE CREVECOER FAMILY					■					
BISHOPS OF ROCHESTER & ARCHBISHOP OF CANTERBURY						■				
KING HENRY VIII							■			
THE SIDNEY FAMILY								■		
THE PORTER FAMILY									■	
THE MORLAND FAMILY										■

MAJOR LAMBERHURST INDUSTRIES IN HISTORY

CENTURY	700	800	900	1000	1100	1200	1300	1400	1500	1600	1700	1800	1900	2000
INDUSTRY														
SWINE FATTENING	■	■	■	■	■									
WOOL					■	■	■							
WATER MEADOW GRASS					■	■	■							
MILLING						■	■	■	■	■	■	■		
CLOTH MANUFACTURE							■	■	■	■				
LEATHER							■	■						
CATTLE MARKET							■	■	■	■	■			
SLAUGHTER HOUSE								■				■		
CATTLE								■	■	■	■	■		
IRON MANUFACTURE									■	■				
HOP GROWING									■	■	■	■		
BREWING							■	■	■	■	■	■	■	
BAKING							■	■	■	■	■	■	■	■

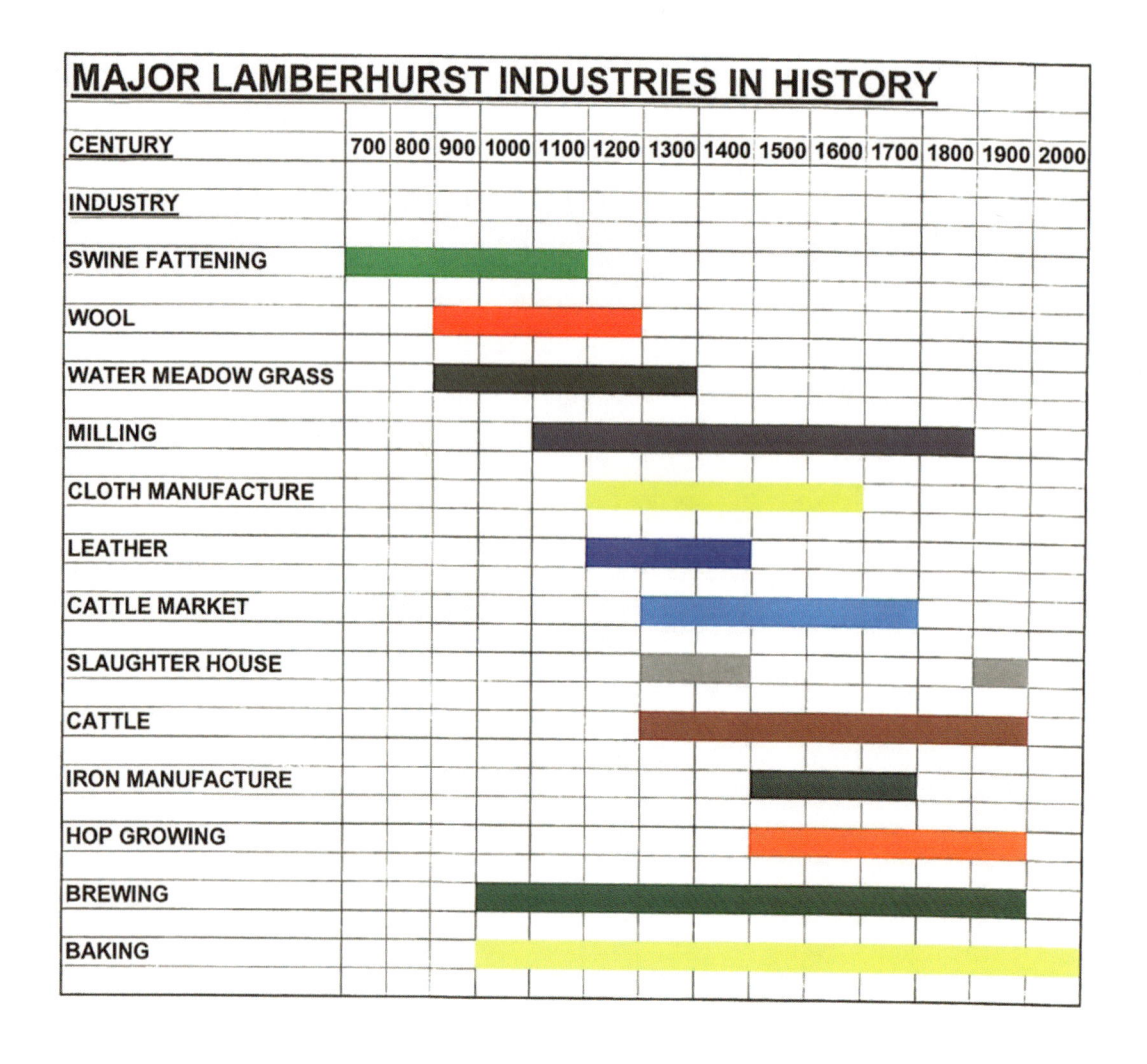

HISTORICAL LOCATION CHART – BAKING

THE BAKING INDUSTRY OF LAMBERHURST CIRCA 1550

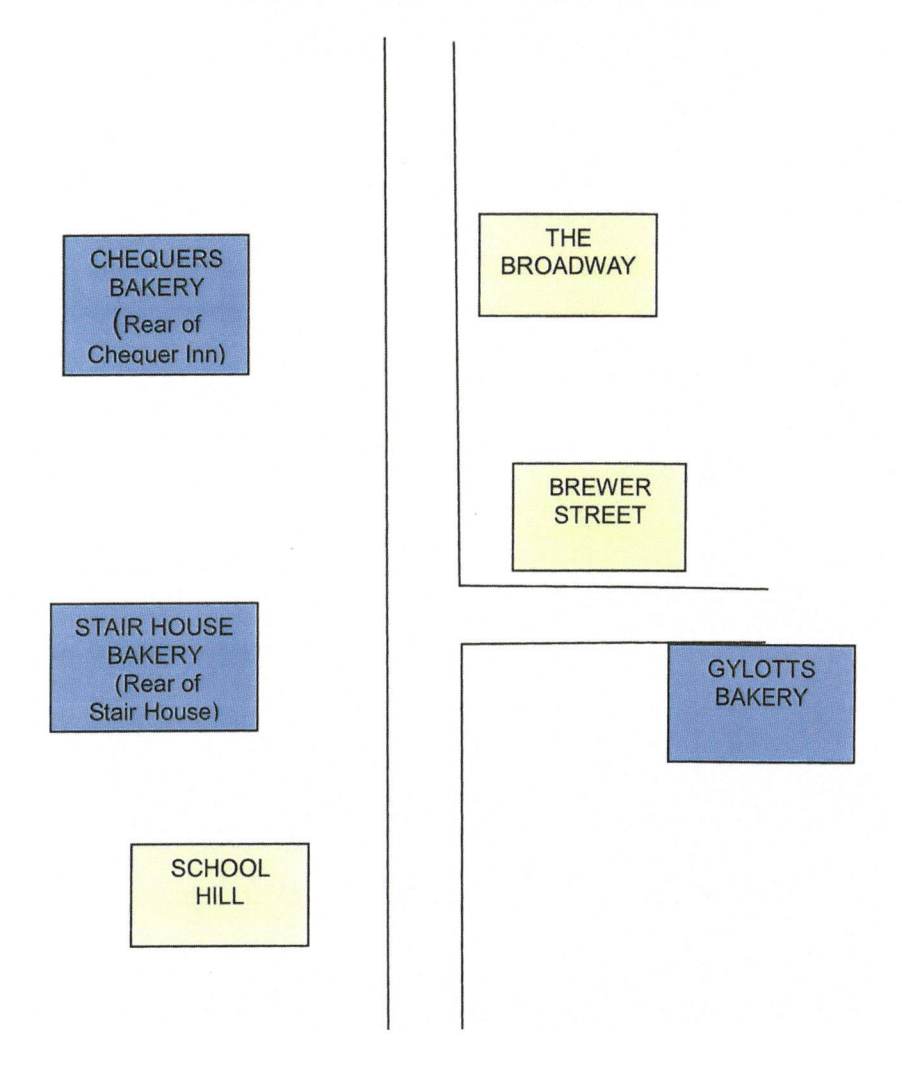

- CHEQUERS BAKERY (Rear of Chequer Inn)
- THE BROADWAY
- BREWER STREET
- STAIR HOUSE BAKERY (Rear of Stair House)
- GYLOTTS BAKERY
- SCHOOL HILL

HISTORICAL LOCATION CHART – CLOTH

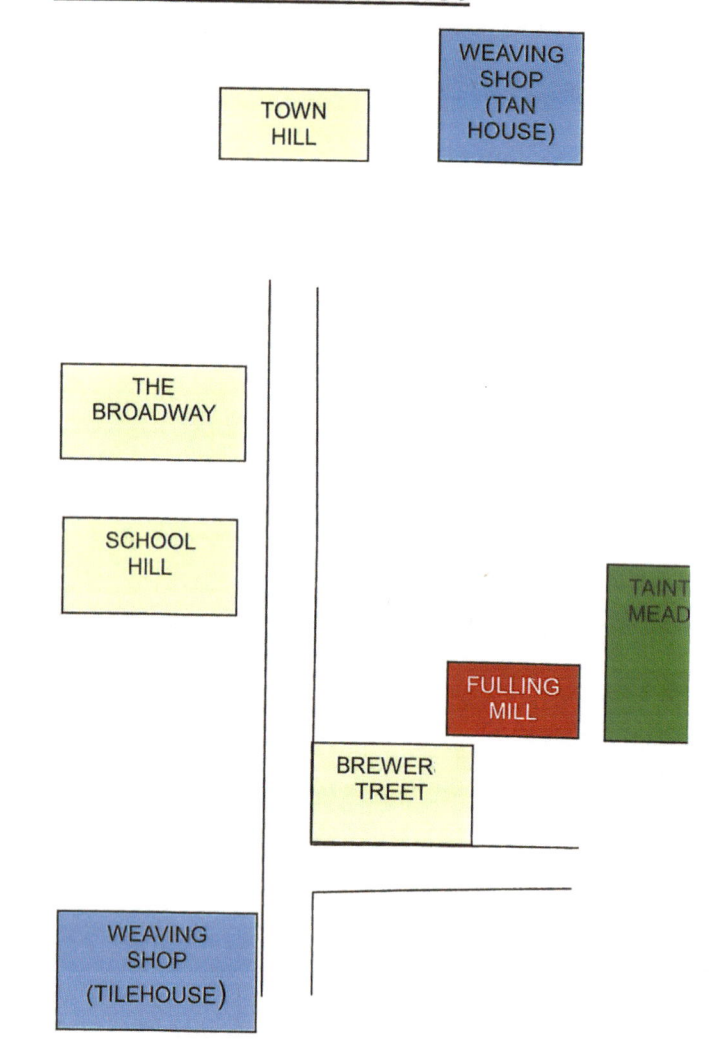

THE CLOTH INDUSTRY OF LAMBERHURST CIRCA 1550

- TOWN HILL
- WEAVING SHOP (TAN HOUSE)
- THE BROADWAY
- SCHOOL HILL
- TAINT MEAD
- FULLING MILL
- BREWER TREET
- WEAVING SHOP (TILEHOUSE)

HISTORICAL LOCATION CHART – LEATHER

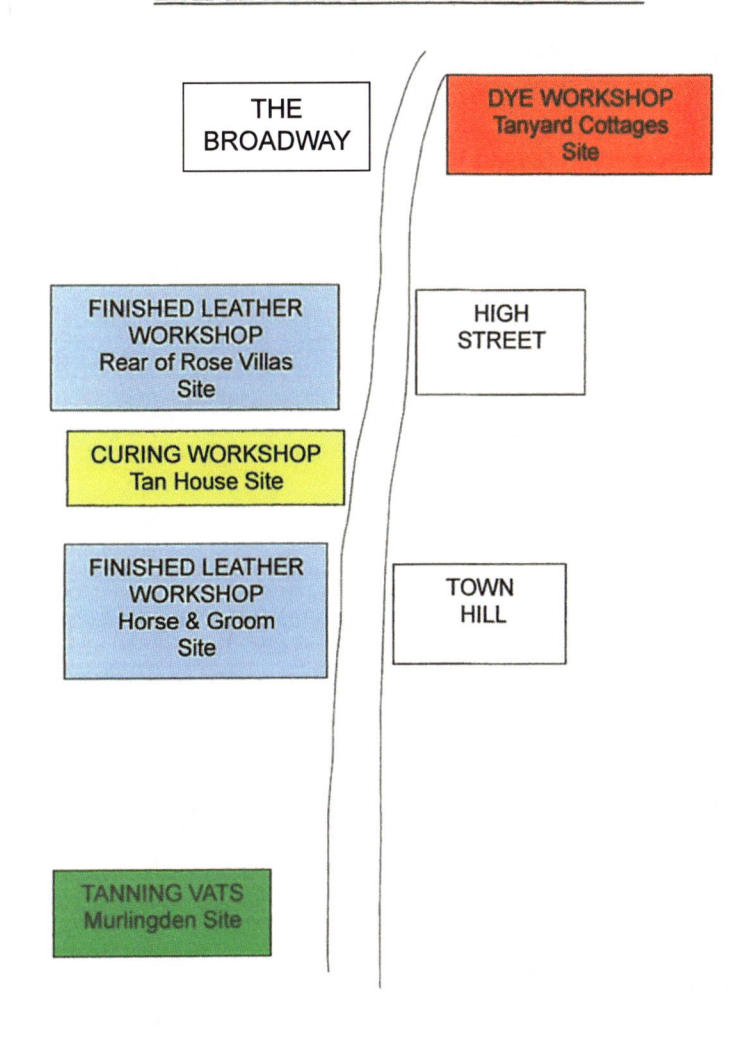

THE LEATHER INDUSTRY OF LAMBERHURST CIRCA 1550

- THE BROADWAY
- DYE WORKSHOP — Tanyard Cottages Site
- FINISHED LEATHER WORKSHOP — Rear of Rose Villas Site
- HIGH STREET
- CURING WORKSHOP — Tan House Site
- FINISHED LEATHER WORKSHOP — Horse & Groom Site
- TOWN HILL
- TANNING VATS — Murlingden Site

HISTORICAL LOCATION CHART – BREWING

THE BREWING INDUSTRY OF
LAMBERHURST CIRCA 1550

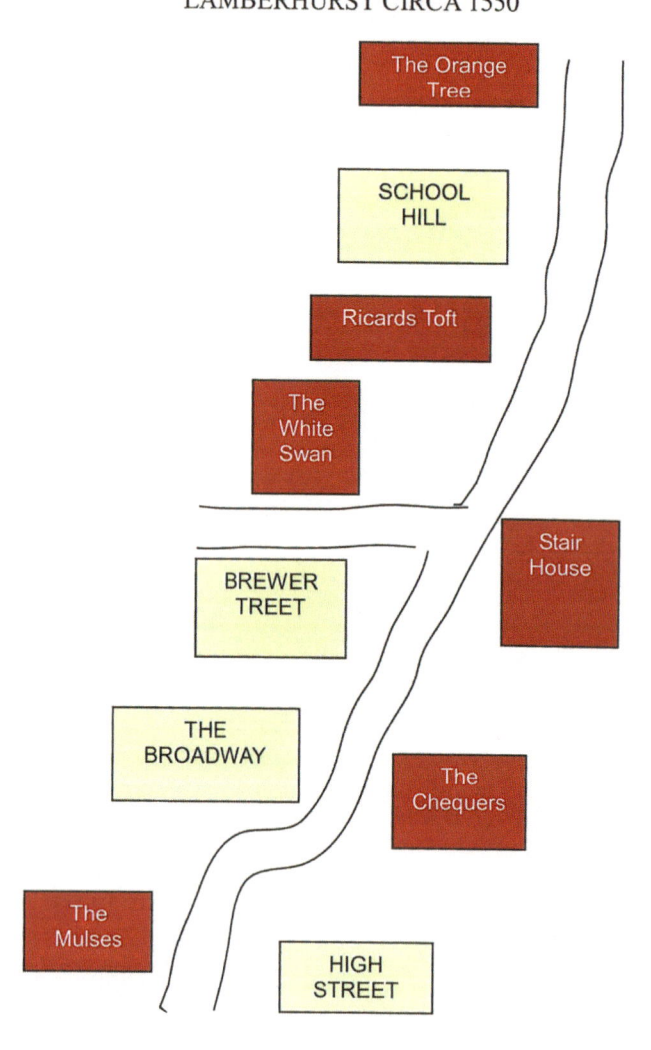

- The Orange Tree
- SCHOOL HILL
- Ricards Toft
- The White Swan
- BREWER TREET
- Stair House
- THE BROADWAY
- The Chequers
- The Mulses
- HIGH STREET

HISTORICAL CHART – OCCUPATIONS 1851

1851 CENSUS OF POPULATION – LAMBERHURST HOUSEHOLDS BY TRADE			
TRADE	TOTAL	KENT SIDE	SUSSEX SIDE
FARM LABOURER	35		
SHOEMAKER	10		
CARPENTER	7		5 MEN, 2 MEN
BREWER	5	10 MEN	FRED SMITH
BLACKSMITH	6		
FARMER	5	103 ACRES, 6 MEN	215 ACRES 11 MEN, 210 ACRES 10 MEN, 70 ACRES 1 MAN, 160 ACRES, 6 MEN
SHOPKEEPER	4		THOMAS TWORT, 22 MEN
PUBLICAN	4		CHEQUERS 150 ACRES, 6 MEN
DRESSMAKER	3		
TAILOR	3		
BREWERS LABOURER	3		
MILLERS LABOURER	3		
BRICKLAYER	3		
BAKER	2		
DOCTOR	2		
PAINTER & GLAZIER	2		
BUTCHER	2	JAMES PIERCE	HENRY ROBERTS
SAWYER	2		
STRAW BONNET MAKER	1		
PAINTER	1		
SAILOR	1		
GROUCER & DRAPER	1		
MASON & BRICKLAYER	1		
WHEELWRIGHT	1		
FELMONGER	1		
PAINTER	1		
FARRIER	1		
SEEDSMAN	1		
GLOVEMAKER	1		
BASKET MAKER	1		
CHIMNEY SWEEP	1		
COOPER	1		
BROOM MAKER	1		
CONFECTIONER	1		
CARRIER	1		
GLOVE MAKER	1		
DRESSMAKER	1		
SOLICITOR	1		
WEAVERS LABOURER	1		
BREWING LABOURER	1		
MILLER	1		
HARNESS MAKER	1		
	125		

HISTORICAL CHART – FARMS 1881

LAMBERHURST FARMS – NINETEENTH CENTURY

REF.	FARM NAME	ACREAGE	LABOURERS MEN	LABOURERS BOYS (GIRLS)
6	TUTTYSHAMS	520	15	0
7	BEWL BRIDGE	313	12	3
8	HOATHLY	246	10	4
9	SANDHURST	230	10	2
10	MANORDEN	210	10	0
11	COGGERS	200	10	2
12	DOWNS	200	14	2
13	RIDGE	190	10	0
14	GREAT DUNKS	176	3	2
15	GRANTHAM HALL	170	3	0
16	WALSINGHAMS	160	6	0
17	THE CHEQUERS	150	6	0
18	OWLS HOUSE	104	3	0
19	WINDMILL	102	3	0
20	PITTS GATE	100	4	2
21	LINDRIDGE	95	1	1
22	BEECH	90	3	2
23	MOUNT PLEASANT	80	1	1
24	WHISKETTS	65	3	0
25	MAYNARDS	56	2	0
26	OWLS CASTLE	50	1	1
27	LITTLE LINDRIDGE	45	1	0
28	SPRAY HILL	33	1	0
29	PARSONAGE	30	1	0
30	FURNACE MILL	20	4	0
31	UZZARDS	18	1	0
32	COLD HARBOUR	17	1	1(1)
33	MAITLANDS	16	2	0
	TOTALS	3686	141	24

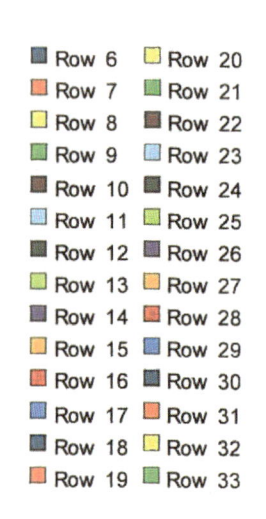

PART 4 – ACKNOWLEDGEMENTS AND REFERENCES

1) John H. Moon: *The Great House, A Brief Early History of Coggers Hall, Lamberhurst & Bygone Lamberhurst, The Dens of Lamberhurst, The Inns of Lamberhurst*
2) Rochester Abbey Records
3) Charter of the Leeds Priory
4) The Court Rolls of Lamberhurst Manor
5) Survey of Lamberhurst Manor for Sir Robert Sidney
6) Archbishop of Canterbury's Custodials
7) Abbot of Robertsbridge Custodials and Land Grants
8) MK Heritage Web site: Odo of Bayeux
9) Medieval Mosaic Web site: The Battle Abbey Roll and Norman Lineage
10) British History On Line: Lamberhurst, Houses of Cistercian Monks, Houses of Austin Canons, The History and Liberty of Rochester, The Priory of Leeds
11) David Nash Ford: *The Royal Berkshire History*
12) Historic UK com: Historic England
13) Wikipedia: Sir Henry Sidney, Sir Robert Sidney, the Morland Dynasty, Grist Mills, Wool, Watches and Clocks
14) John Derrick: *The Image of Irelande*
15) The Morland Family of Westmorland, England Website
16) W. C. Morland: *The Diaries*
17) Chism List (held at The Public Records Office)
18) Home Baking History Website
19) River Wey and Navigations Web site: Flour Milling and the History of Bread
20) English Heritage Web site: Images of England (Crown Copyright).
21) *Pigots Directory* 1840: Lamberhurst
22) The Court Rolls of Hoathly Manor
23) The Wey Valley Clothing Industry: Wool, Linen and Leather
24) Ernest Straker: *Wealden Iron*
25) The RH7 History Group: *Wealden Iron Industry*
26) With acknowledgement to West Sussex County Council, Mike Codd and PPL Limited
27) The Loseley Manuscripts
28) Peter Brandon: *The Kent and Sussex Weald*
29) Exploring 20th Century London Web site: Hop Picking
30) The Museum of Kent Life: Hopping Down in Kent
31) Tunbridge Wells Borough Council: Lamberhurst Conservation Area
32) Peter Sands
33) Will of Lady Hamley
34) Perambulation Charter
35) Will of Nicholas Fowle
36) William Gravett: Unpublished Surveys
37) Michael Zell: *Early Modern Kent*
38) UK National Census: 1881, 1891 and 1901
39) Lamberhurst Village Web site
40) National Archives: Births, Marriages and Deaths and other articles
41) The Shambles, York Web site
42) Turnpike Roads in England Web site
43) Manor of Scotney Custodials

44) The Chequers Inn Web site
45) History AC Web site: Gazetteer of Markets and Fairs – Kent
46) William Morland: *The Church in Lamberhurst* 1770 Map of Lamberhurst
47) Statutes of Edward VI, 5 and 6
48) Lorraine Flisher and Michael Zell: *The Demise of the Kent Broadcloth Industry*
49) Edward Hasted: *The History and Topographical Survey of the County of Kent* Volume 5
50) The Sidney Family Web site
51) Lady Hope: *English Homes and Villages, Kent and Sussex*
52) The Cattle Site Web site – Cattle Breeds Sussex
53) Edlin
54) Wealden Buildings Study Group
55) Absolute Astronomy Web site: Fulling
56) Witheridge Web site: Fulling
57) Fulling Mills of the Isle of Wight Web site
58) Beef Shorthorn Breed History Web site
59) Mr N. Morland
60) Thomas Walker Horsfield: *The History, Antiquities and Topography of the County of Suffolk*
61) Kelly: *Directory of Kent*
62) Walter Jerrold: *Highways and Byways of Kent*
63) Marjorie Edwards
64) The Gurr Family History Web site
65) Combwell Custodials and Land Grants
66) Mr Basil Matthews
67) William Clout: *Map of The Manor of Lamberhurst*
68) Barbara Uren
69) Nancy Gurr
70) Elizabeth Bullock
71) Hampshire County Council: *The Conservation of Water Meadow Structures*
72) Charles Igglesden: *A Saunter Through Kent*
73) Thomas Benge Burr: *The History of Tunbridge Wells*
74) Brenda Kennard
75) Phyllis Kennard: *A Lamberhurst Lass*
76) 1770 Map of Lamberhurst
77) *The Poll Book for Knights of the Shire, Kent*
78) Lamberhurst Historical Society Private Photographic Collection (by kind permission)
79) Plea Roll 1241
80) Mr K. McAlpine
81) Mr W. F. Warren
82) The Porter Family Web site
83) Derby Museum and Art Gallery
84) Jeremy Hodgkinson

Special thanks to Barbara Uren of the Lamberhurst Historical Society for her help, guidance and support

INDEX

A
Abbots of Robertsbridge 3,4,10-11,26,37
Aethelbald 6-7
Animal Husbandry 45-46
Annual Fair 46-47
Archbishop of Canterbury 3,10-12,26,29,42,45,46
Asserters 10
Avard John 26-27

B
Baking 25-27
Ballard Joseph 65
Benge William 56
Begebury 4
Beer 38-40
Bell Inn (The)
Bishop Eu 1,45
Bishop Odo 1,4,8-9
Bishops of Rochester 7
Bread 25-27
Brewer Street 39,61
Brewing 37-41
Broadway (The) 47
Butchers 67-68

C
Cannon 52,52,58
Cattle 45-46
Cattle Market 46-48
Cawerden Thomas Sir 55
Chafery 52-53
Chequers Farm 60-61
Chemical Manufacture 67
Church Glebe 3
Cider 37-38
Clock and Watch Makers 65
Cloth Manufacture 42-45
Cogger Robert 42,45
Collyn Alexander 55
Collyn Steven 55-56
Construction 65-66
Corn Milling 27-29
Curing 48
Curtehope 3

D
de Crevecoeur Daniel 10
de Crevecoeur Emma 24,46
de Crevecoeur Hamo 9,11,29
de Crevecoeur Helyas 25,37
de Crevecoeur Robert 1,9,25,27,45
Delamain Colonel 31
Dens of Lamberhurst 1-4,20
de Scotney 3
Down The 23,62
Down Farm 62

E
East Lindhryeg 1
East Mill 27-30
Evans William 73-74
Everheste 3-4

F
Finished Leather 49
Filmer Edward Sir 56
Fire back 56
Forstall Farm 64
Fulling 42-45
Fulling Mill 43-45
Furnace Mill 33-35

G
Gerelody 37
Gill Stream 43-45
Gott Peter 56-57
Great Brooms Island 9,27,29
Great Dens 1
Great Ditch The 52
Grist Mill 27
Gurr Ernie 69-70
Gurr William 68-69,73

H
Hansfleote/Hanslake 1,21-22
Hayden 4
Hoathly 3,23,50,55-57
Hoathly Mill 33-35
Hop Growing 60-64
Hop Pickers 62-64
Hop string Manufacture 66

I
Iron Smelting and Manufacturer 50-59

K
Kentish Broadcloth 42

Kersey Cloth 42

L
Lady Meade 22,42
Lamberhurst Farms C16th – Size and Crops 15
Lamberhurst Farms C19th – Crops 18
Lamberhurst Furnace and Forge 51-59
Leather 48-50
Leeds Priory 9,26,29
Lindhryeg 1
Little Dens 1
Lords of the Manor 5-19

M
Marshall's Abattoir 47
Mill Bay 30
Molts The 38
Morland Henry Colonel 18-19,73
Morland Thomas 16
Morland William 15-16
Morland William Alexander 16
Morland William Courtney 16-18,62
Mulsa 38
Mulses The 38

O
Oven Door 56
Owling 24

P
Pannage 20
Pepper Mill 35-36
Pepper Rent 36
Porter John 15

R
Padgham Edward 31
Red Cows 45
Reeve George and Charlie 71
Reeves Benjamin 65
Reynold Walter 11-12,46
Robertsbridge Abbey 30
Rumens Thomas 65

S
Saddlers 66
Sands Peter 70-71
Shambles (The) 48
Sheep 23,25
Sidney Henry Sir 13
Sidney Philip Sir 14
Sidney Robert Sir 13-14

Sidney William Sir 13
Slaughter Houses 20-21,47
Smiths Brewery 38
Smith & Co 38-40
Smith & Simpson 38
Spinning 43
Survey of Lamberhurst 1,29
Swine Fattening 20

T
Taint Mead 44
Tanning 48,50
Tentering 44
Tentering Hooks 44
Tithe 12
Town Mill 9,30-31
Town Windmill 31-33
Tuttyshams 3

W
Wash fold 23
Water Meadows 21-23
Weaving 43
Weekly Market 12,46-47
Whisketts Farm 62
Wellere William Sir 56
West Mill 9,30-31
Wic 25
Winder Arthur 66
Wine 40-41
Wool 23-25

CPSIA information can be obtained
at www.ICGtesting.com
Printed in the USA
2536LVUK00005B